Mining the Future The Bafokeng Story

Researched, written and edited by Totem Media
for the Research & Planning Department of
the Royal Bafokeng Administration

THE BAFOKENG
STORY IS AN
EXTRAORDINARY
STORY

Our ancestors have achieved extraordinary things that continue to inspire us to imagine an extraordinary future. As a result of their foresight we own an extraordinary piece of land. Some of our elders tell us that we chose a valley that gathered heavy dew during the night. This dew was interpreted as a promise of a fertile land and prosperous future. This is why we are called Bafokeng, the people of the dew. Our name is a promise, a future foretold.

The land has been good to us. It has offered fertile soil for grazing and agriculture. It has even offered up its mineral riches to us. Running under it is the richest known reserve of platinum in the world. We are a small community, but the wisdom of our ancestors and the fortune of our platinum have allowed us to dream big dreams.

It has not been easy to keep our land. We have had to fight for it and work for it. All through our history we have had to resist invaders who have tried to take our land away from us.

In the mid-19th century, one of our great leaders, Kgosi (King) Mokgatle, made the decision to buy the land, even though it was already ours. He did this so that it would be ours legally in the eyes of the Boers of the Transvaal Republic.

Many Bafokeng have made sacrifices so that we could keep and enjoy our land today. In the late 1800s our young men went to work on mines to raise the money to pay for our land. Many years later, Bafokeng men and women stood together to resist the forces of apartheid that drove us into the bantustan of Bophuthatswana. We even had to fight the mining industry to keep our rights to the mineral wealth of our land. Through all of this we held on to the promise of the dew.

Today the Bafokeng people, known as the Royal Bafokeng Nation (RBN), own 1400 square kilometres of land in North West Province between the Magaliesberg Nature Reserve and Rustenburg in the south, and Sun City and the Vaalkop Nature Reserve in the north. About 300 000 people live in the territory. Just more than half are Bafokeng.

A lot changed for us when in 1999 a nine-year legal battle between the Royal Bafokeng Nation and Impala Platinum was settled out of court in favour of giving us significant platinum royalties. We have used these royalties and shares in platinum companies to create and manage community development. The Royal Bafokeng Nation ensures that all Bafokeng households, in the 29 villages, have access to water, electricity, roads, health care and education.

While platinum has given us advantages, we know that it will run out and that we cannot be dependent on platinum alone. It is very important that we diversify our economy and provide the kind of educational opportunities that will help our people enter the local, national and global economy.

The Royal Bafokeng Nation has grown into one of South Africa's best examples of the sustainable use of mineral resources. We want our learning journey to generate models of best practice for other developing communities.

You might ask, 'What exactly can a Bafokeng model offer communities that do not have access to the same kind of wealth?' We do recognise that we are not like anyone else. We have unusual resources. But the model we offer others is not just about money. It is about the way we have committed ourselves to a long view of the future. It is also about the way we deliberately embrace tradition as a medium for managing conflict and change.

Some say we are lucky. But it is what we do with our luck that counts.

Through the responsible investment of our assets, the education of our people, the development of our villages, and an inspiring vision of the future, we will continue to fulfil the promise; we will continue to be the people of the dew – Bafokeng.

EVEN WITH EXTRAORDINARY RESOURCES THERE ARE NO EASY ANSWERS

The success of platinum has created high expectations among our people, but we are learning to accept that even with our wealth there are no easy answers to the challenges of development.

If the current wealth of the Royal Bafokeng Nation was divided up among community members it would allow people to maintain their current lifestyle and expenses for the next fifty years. Then we would run out of money. For this reason wealth has to be invested on behalf of the nation and distributed strategically if it is to grow for our children's children. For people who have needs that they want to see addressed immediately, taking the long view is not always popular.

Money cannot, on its own, ensure sustainable prosperity and success for the Bafokeng people. This requires a willingness to learn, the skills of critical and creative thinking, accountable leadership, meaningful political representation, a focus on development, a commitment to education, gender equity, opportunities for new businesses to grow, and care for the environment.

Success also requires something that has very rarely been achieved anywhere in the world – a dynamic and mutually beneficial relationship between the capitalist values of individuality and the traditional value of holding the community in higher esteem than the self. Are we foolish to believe that the two can coexist in a kind of 'social capitalism'

where entrepreneurial drive seeks to benefit and inspire a community instead of an individual?

On the one hand, communities need schools, roads, water and street lights. On the other hand, individuals need student loans, opportunities for new businesses and career paths within our Bafokeng institutions.

We do not want to create a culture of dependency. We want to create a culture and an environment in which communities and individuals are encouraged to stand on their own feet and take control of their future.

To do this, we have embraced an integrated strategy called Vision 2020 – our plan for mining the future.

IN ORDER TO CREATE YOUR FUTURE YOU NEED TO UNDERSTAND YOUR PAST

Many people have said, 'In order to create your future you need to understand your past.'

This is not always easy, as history is represented in many different ways and according to many different agendas. What we hear from historians and archaeologists does not always agree with what we have been told by our storytellers, praise singers and elders. Evidence comes to us in many different forms. There are ancient artefacts found by archaeologists and there are stories passed down through many generations. There are visual records like graveyards, photographs and video archives. There are written documents like historical records, title deeds and minutes from meetings. There are personal perspectives like published biographies and spoken eyewitness accounts. Evidence is even contained in artistic traditions like architecture and pottery. Making sense of all the evidence is one of the challenges facing us.

History is also not always positive and affirming. It may confront us with things our people did that we would rather not remember. But we don't want to invent a version of the past that suits us or makes us look good. We want to learn from the experience of others and build on the gains of the past.

A typical Sotho-Tswana homestead from the 1800s

One of the things we have inherited from our ancestors is our totem, the symbol of our people – the crocodile. While some other Tswana groups also have a crocodile as their totem, our crocodile is unique because it is the only one with a closed mouth. This is usually interpreted as a symbol of peace and is linked to the way our ancestors were often diplomatic rather than antagonistic. The closed-mouth crocodile could also be read as our willingness to listen, watch and learn, instead of acting impulsively.

**A PROUD
TRADITION OF
COMMUNITY
PARTICIPATION**

One of the things we have inherited from our ancestors is our traditional system of hereditary leadership. This system has been criticised as authoritarian, sexist and undemocratic. We think it offers some important advantages.

Our leaders cannot run away from their responsibility. They have to work with their people to address the issues of the day. They cannot benefit themselves for a term and then move on, unaccountable for the damage they have caused. They are not promoted out of their jobs when they do not perform. Our hereditary leaders, like the Kgosi (King) and the dikgosana (traditional headmen), are 'leaders for life'.

Our leaders are also accessible. We have a long and proud tradition of community participation in decision making and planning. There are 72 wards, or makgotla, that span the 29 Bafokeng villages. The 72 traditional headmen, or dikgosana, are responsible for their makgotla where local people raise local issues. Makgotla take place at least once a month to debate and create solutions. Twice a year the whole community is invited to Kgotha Kgothe, a gathering of the Bafokeng people. At Kgotha Kgothe any adult Mofokeng can raise issues, ask questions, put forward proposals and vote. These opportunities allow Bafokeng people to communicate with their leaders and participate actively in decision-making processes.

A typical lekgotla or community meeting.

In 2009 the members of the
Supreme Council visited the
South African Parliament
and participated in portfolio
subcommittees. This
experience prepared them
for more focused roles in
the portfolio subcommittees
in the Supreme Council.

Our leaders are part of a tradition that tries to build on what has come before. We do not find ourselves in the position where every few years new leaders try to start everything from scratch just so that they can be seen to be the authors of new projects.

Our leaders are life-long learners. The chairpersons, treasurers and secretaries of makgotla are being trained in management and communication skills. Our dikgosana attend regular training courses on key issues like leadership, financial planning, HIV and global warming.

The Royal Bafokeng Nation is led by Kgosi Leruo T. Molotlegi. He assumed the role of kgosi after his brother Kgosi Lebone II died in 2000.

While the Kgosi is the supreme head of the Bafokeng Nation, he cannot act outside certain checks and balances. He must act within the consensus of the Supreme Council, which consists of all the hereditary headmen, five elected officials and five officials nominated by the Kgosi. He also receives feedback through the makgotla and Kgotha Kgothe.

CLOSING THE GENERATION GAP

One of the challenges facing our traditional structures is the inclusion of young people.

They are the future leaders of our people. In the old days, they would slowly be integrated into decision-making processes over many years, first performing practical duties in their makgotla and only then, after proving themselves as loyal and reliable, would they be included in more important discussions. Today our education system encourages young people to think for themselves – and so they should, as they have so many more complex choices facing them. They are also skilled in using communication technologies that link them to a global culture. They often have access to more information than their own parents and dikgosana. Times have changed. We must find new ways to prepare them for leadership and responsibility. Young people have great energy and new ways of seeing things. Their ideas and innovative approaches are some of our most important assets as a community.

Many of our young people travel far away from our territory and far away from our customs and traditions. We are slowly learning that when we meet up with them again, we need to learn from where they have been and what they have seen. We need to ask them to tell the stories of their adventures so that we can all benefit from what they have experienced – and so that we can offer them encouragement and support. They can light the path to the future and share the best that the world has to offer, in the spirit of Vision 2020.

One purpose of Kgotha Kgothe is to update people on a wide range of developments It can at times feel like a series of formal reports rather than a discussion. For this reason we have begun regional forms of Kgotha Kgothe, which will give more people, including the youth, the opportunity to be actively involved in the decisions that affect their lives. **No one has a greater investment in the challenges that face us than our young people.** They are the ones who will have to deal with the consequences of decisions made today.

'YOU DON'T HAVE TO AGREE WITH ME POLITICALLY TO WORK WITH ME.'

Bernard Makgaka is a dynamic youth leader. He encourages young people to get involved in the politics of Bafokeng life by attending community meetings and talking to the dikgosana. 'I am Tswana but I am Mofokeng first. I know how to raise issues – even if I don't agree, I still show respect.'

This does not mean that he is afraid to express critical points of view. He is calling for more Bafokeng graduates to be absorbed into institutions of the Royal Bafokeng Nation and for increased support for young professionals.

Bernard is a graduate of Thethe High School and completed a BComm (Accounting) at the University of Johannesburg. He has returned to participate in the creation of the Bafokeng future. 'Young people get educated but they are not motivated to come back. I came back because I wanted to make sure my voice was heard. You can't just complain.'

He has been active in the ANC Youth League and in non-political local community youth structures. His message to young people is: 'Don't wait for the Kgosi to save you. Take charge of your own future.'

Take charge of your own future

Gabriel Lenkwe encourages young people to attend their makgotla. 'I attend lekgotla in my village. People who attend are teachers, lawyers, professors – but once they are there they listen to the kgosana (traditional headman). They forget about their professions and respect the kgosana. Part of my being there is not to change their mind but to learn about what they are doing. Learn how the system works by listening.'

Gabriel is the Youth Programme Coordinator based at the Bafokeng Youth Centre in Luka. He coordinates youth programmes in all 29 Bafokeng villages and is committed to giving young people a voice in community affairs.

Gabriel cites alcohol abuse as the biggest challenge facing young people. He explains how butchers and liquor stores go hand in hand, providing areas for people to drink and braai. While these are opportunities for entrepreneurs, alcohol abuse leads to domestic violence, teenage pregnancies, sexually transmitted infections and a lack of motivation.

'I got a bursary – it is important for me to plough back. People worked hard for this land. As young people we need to do the same thing.'

Learn how the system works by listening

'Opportunities are there but we need to change our mindset.'

THE BAFOKENG
ARE A VERY
ANCIENT TRIBE
BUT OUR TRUE
ORIGINS ARE
HOTLY DEBATED

Molokwane,
a Bakwena settlement
occupied between
the late 18th century and
early 19th century.

Naboth Mokgatle, grandson of Kgosi Mokgatle, wrote this about the origins of the Bafokeng:

❝ Our tribal symbol is a crocodile (kwena) and we call ourselves and are known as Bakwena ... All I know because of the legend, which was handed down by the old to the young, is that from Lesotho my people went to Botswana. Their headquarters was Molepolole. They moved away, led by a man called Tshukudu whom they made their Chief as they moved south-eastward, and crossed the Madikwe River into the Transvaal. Tshukudu and his people moved on until they reached the mountains today known as Pilanesberg mountains ... They reached a place called Mogoase where they settled down ... At Mogoase, my ancestors' first settlement as an independent tribe, they flourished and their wealth increased. They had the whole field open to them, their animals grazed anywhere they chose, and they hunted everywhere at will ... They travelled far afield without coming into contact with other tribes and therefore made the whole land they travelled theirs. Because of the polygamous system they practised, the tribe grew, and they went on cherishing the crocodile symbol they adopted from their ancestors in Molepolole. ❞

THE BAFOKENG
ARE A VERY
ANCIENT TRIBE
BUT OUR TRUE
ORIGINS ARE
HOTLY DEBATED

Marothodi,
a Batlokwa settlement
occupied between
the late 18th century and
early 19th century.

Before the 19th century concepts such as 'Sotho', 'Tswana', 'Pedi' and 'Ndebele' did not exist as group identities.

According to some archaeologists, such as Tom Huffman, the Fokeng were a dynamic grouping of many diverse people. This grouping originally came from northern Natal, with Nguni roots. Over time they adopted Tswana culture and eventually split into the Bafokeng, the Bapo and the Batlokwa. These groups were the ones who brought the technology of stonewalling into the area of the present North West Province.

Part of Huffman's evidence is a particular kind of pottery, known as Ntsuanatsatsi pottery. It is found at sites in the north-eastern Free State and the Rustenburg area and links the Fokeng to the inland move-ment of some Nguni.

If Huffman is correct, then our ancestors were not linked to the Bakwena as so many oral traditions suggest. His interpretation of the evidence does, however, let us make the proud claim that our ancestors pioneered stonewalling in the Rustenburg area between 1450 and 1500. By about 1780 this technology was used to build the impressive Tswana stone settlements like Molokwane (a Bakwena site) and Marothodi (a Batlokwa site). These each housed over 20 000 people two hundred and thirty years ago.

It seems that in the years leading up to 1750 the Bahurutshe were the dominant group in the Rustenburg–Marico area. They were regarded as the senior clan of all the Tswana groups. This didn't stop the Bafokeng questioning their authority. The land the Bafokeng occupied was, as it is to this day, surrounded by mountains. For this reason they were unable to expand in any direction and needed to engage in conflicts over resources.

From the middle of the 1700s onwards the area was a 'hot spot' of low-level conflicts. Under the leadership of the great warrior chief, Kgosi Sekete IV, the Bafokeng experienced conflicts with the Bakwena, the Batlokwa, the Bakgatla-ba-Kgafela and the Bapo.

Kgosi Sekete IV was succeeded by Thethe. While at war with the Bakgatla-ba-Kgafela, Kgosi Thethe faced a challenge from his two brothers, Nameng and Noge. He sought the help of the Bapedi. The Bapedi king Sekwete sent his brother Malekutu to assist Kgosi Thethe. But Malekutu did not defeat Nameng, and he took many Bafokeng men, women, children and cattle into captivity.

A HOT SPOT O CONFLICTS

Nameng was eventually killed in a battle with the Bammatau. Noge assumed power over the majority of the Bafokeng, and Kgosi Thethe fled with his wife and son Mokgatle and sought refuge among the Bammatau.

At this time Thethe made the following prophecy: 'If you kill me, the Bafokeng will be scattered. First will come the red ants to destroy you, then will come the black ants which will also destroy you; lastly the yellow ants and an animal without a cloven hoof will appear.'

While the Batlokwa and Bakgatla-ba-Kgafela became the powerful Tswana groups in the area, it was the Bapedi, under Thulare, that took advantage of the conflict between Tswana groups to dominate the area. According to legend the Bapedi were the red ants that Kgosi Thethe spoke of in his prophecy.

But the dominance of the Bapedi did not last long. In 1824 the Bakololo, under Sebetwane, invaded the area. They, in turn, were defeated by new invaders – the Ndebele under Mzilikazi in 1830. It is commonly believed that the Ndebele were the black ants of Thethe's prophecy.

Mzilikazi, in turn, was defeated in 1837 by the Boers – the yellow ants?

AND CHALLENGES

Our history has been a battle for power in our area. Through it all, kgosi after kgosi has helped us keep our land and our name.

Our Queen Mother, Semane Molotlegi, has said: 'Every kgosi is building on the previous kgosi – hopefully we can do it forever.'

The uncle of our current kgosi, Rre Magosi Tumagole, has said: 'Succession is like a relay race. One kgosi hands over the baton to the next.'

Tshukudu
Nape
Setsetse
Mmutle
Phôgôlê
Maree
Maelangwe
Maleriba
Kgualu (Kgulo)
Modubiane
Phate
Maphate
Mafole
Mekgise
Morapide
Mpuru
Ntsuane
Ramorwa I
Sekete I
Fokeng
Ramorwa II
Sekete II
Mogono
Magobe (Bogobe)
Monwe

According to P.L. Breutz in his book *The Tribes of Rustenburg and Pilanesberg Districts* (1953), this is the list of Bafokeng dikgosi (kings) from Tshukudu to the beginning of the 18th century.

Sekete III
early 18th century, perhaps at Boschpoort

Diale
mid-18th century, perhaps at Boschpoort

Ramorwa
mid-18th century, Phokeng

Sekete IV
late 18th century, Phokeng

Katane
early 19th century, Phokeng

Thethe (Makgongwana)
early 19th century, Phokeng

Nameng
1820s, Phokeng

Noge
1820s, Phokeng

Mokgatle
1834 – 1891, Phokeng

James Tumagole
1891 – 1896, Phokeng

August Lebone Molotlegi
1896 – 1938, Phokeng

James Manotshe Molotlegi
1938 – 1956, Phokeng

Edward Lebone Molotlegi
1956 – 1995, Phokeng

Lebone Mollwane Molotlegi
1995 – 2000, Phokeng

Leruo Tshekedi Molotlegi
2000 – present, Phokeng

Kgosi Sekete III, from the early 18th century, is the first kgosi in the line that is directly linked to our current kgosi, Leruo Tshekedi Molotlegi, by blood.

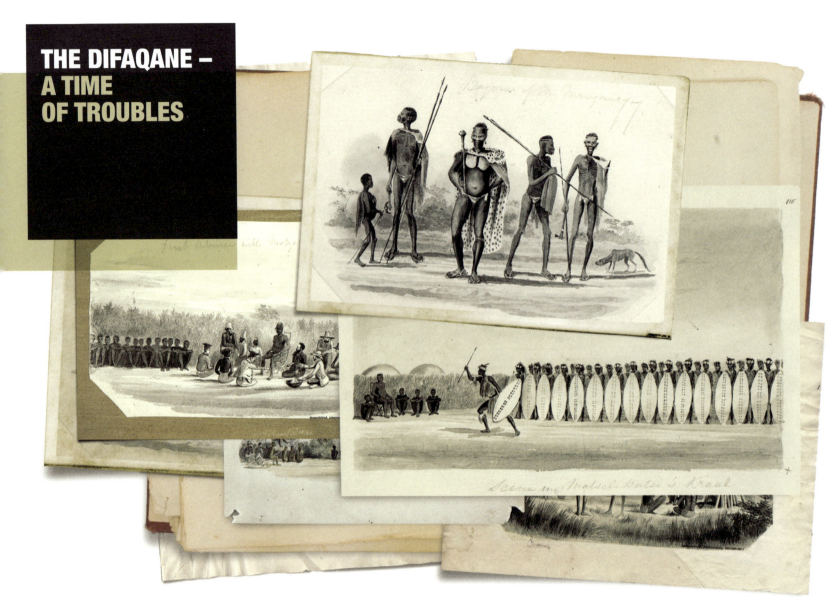

THE DIFAQANE – A TIME OF TROUBLES

Difaqane literally means 'the scattering of the people'. In this period, between about 1822 and 1837, the whole of southern Africa saw huge changes. Drought had left large areas of land empty. Communities were battling over scarce resources such as water, land, cattle and grazing. Stronger communities conquered weaker ones in battle and the weaker communities fled and settled elsewhere, sometimes reorganising themselves into bigger groups that could defend their interests. European missionaries, Dutch settlers and British soldiers were all putting different kinds of pressure on the interior. On top of all of this, the demand for labour from white colonists created both challenges and opportunities that changed the political and economic landscape.

The part of this conflict that had the greatest impact on the Bafokeng was the arrival of the Bakololo under their leader Sebetwane in 1824. The Bakololo were originally part of the Bafokeng but had split off. The Bafokeng suffered terribly under Sebetwane. Whole towns and fields were abandoned as they tried to escape his cruelty.

Sebetwane was defeated by Mzilikazi in 1830. Mzilikazi had fled the Zulu kingdom after defying Shaka's authority.

Noge, who was kgosi of the Bafokeng at the time, killed nine of Mzilikazi's messengers, sparking a battle with Mzilikazi. Noge fled to Thaba N'chu where he remained until his death in 1832. Mzilikazi set up an Ndebele kingdom in the region. After this period the Bafokeng were a scattered people.

It was Mokgatle, the son of Kgosi Thethe, who had been living in exile, who would end the conflict and embrace an attitude of diplomacy when he returned to Phokeng.

[Top] Refugees fleeting from Mzilikazi during the Difaqane.
[Bottom] Mzilikazi's warriors.

THE FATHER OF THE BAFOKENG NATION

Mokgatle is recognised as the father of the Bafokeng nation because he united the Bafokeng people and brought them back to Phokeng after the Difaqane, when he and his mother returned from exile in 1836. He walked from tribe to tribe gathering his people.

Even in the early days of his reign Mokgatle displayed those qualities for which he would be remembered: diplomacy, wisdom and the foresight to collect wealth and land for the Bafokeng that would ensure their future. By entering into a diplomatic relationship with Mzilikazi, he ended the conflict between the Bafokeng and the Ndebele. Mzilikazi allowed him to gather his people and keep cattle. But with the arrival of the Voortrekkers in the Pilanesberg district Mokgatle realised that he had to form a new set of diplomatic relations. In 1837 the Bafokeng helped the Voortrekkers to defeat Mzilikazi. Mzilikazi and his followers moved north and settled in what is today Zimbabwe.

The Voortrekkers used their victory against Mzilikazi to lay claim to the area. Andries Potgieter settled near Phokeng in 1837. Mokgatle welcomed Potgieter to the area and took great care to establish friendly relations with the Boers right from the outset.

Kgosi Mokgatle and one of his wives.

The Boers rewarded the Bafokeng for helping them fight Mzilikazi by giving them a gift of land: the farm Kookfontein 265. The idea that land could be transferred in this way was foreign to the Bafokeng. Kgosi Mokgatle began to realise that the rules of land ownership were changing dramatically, and that they would now have to secure their own land in non-traditional ways – ways that the Boers would understand.

The Bafokeng had been fortunate in their choice of land. The Rustenburg valley held fertile soil, predicable rainfall and good sources of water. After Kgosi Mokgatle brought the tribe back together they were able to settle down and start building a thriving agricultural economy with crops and cattle. But with the arrival of white settlers in the Rustenburg area the position of local communities became increasingly insecure.

SHIFTS IN LAND OWNERSHIP

Up to that point Bafokeng law and custom viewed land as belonging to the community and not to any one individual. Now every (white) citizen of the Transvaal Republic could claim a farm of 3000 morgen and the magistrate would issue a certificate of registration for that land. Such land claims took much of the land historically occupied by the Bafokeng and other black communities.

A Boer camp in the Rustenburg area.

SHIFTS IN POWER

Kgosi Mokgatle had watched how power in the area shifted from one invader to the next: from the Bapedi to the Bakololo to the Ndebele to the Boers. The British were next to assume control of the area north of the Vaal River.

In 1848 the British defeated the Voortrekkers under Andries Pretorius at Boomplaats in the Orange Free State. Pretorius fled to an area outside Pretoria and in 1849 established a Volksraad (a community council) for the Transvaal region. This gave him a mandate to negotiate a political settlement with the British for Boers north of the Vaal River. By 1850 the British had no real interest in the Transvaal (this was before the discovery of gold and diamonds). At the Sand River Convention of 1852 Britain gave the Transvaal Boers the right to govern themselves. Britain abandoned its agreements with black chiefs and gave the Boers political power and access to ammunition. The Zuid-Afrikaansche Republiek (ZAR), also known as the Transvaal, was thus established in 1852. Britain insisted that slavery would not be permitted in the ZAR.

By the middle of the 1800s all the land forming the greater Rustenburg area had been granted to Boer settlers and registered in their names. In June 1855 the Transvaal Volksraad passed a resolution stating: 'no one who is not a recognised burgher shall have any right to possess immovable property in freehold … All coloured persons are excluded herefrom, and the burgher-right may never be granted or allowed to them.' By the 1860s the Bafokeng were left with no land to legally call their own.

But Kgosi Mokgatle used every opportunity arising from the arrival of the Boers to maintain the Bafokeng's hold on their land. The Bafokeng provided a much-needed source of labour to white farmers. They were also drawn into Boer raids on weaker Tswana communities, often with the purpose of capturing children to use as bonded labourers (*inboekselinge*). In exchange for their assistance and cooperation, the Boers gave guns to the

Bafokeng, which allowed them to participate in the ivory trade in the area. At that time it was unheard of for Boers to give guns to a local Bantu-speaking group.

Some thirty years after Mokgatle brought his people back to Phokeng, the Bafokeng were thriving, having built up their wealth through cattle, crops, guns, ivory, labour and land – land that did not yet formally belong to them.

THE RELATIONSHIP BETWEEN THE BAFOKENG AND THE CHRISTIAN MISSIONARIES

It was during Kgosi Mokgatle's reign that missionaries first came to settle among the Bafokeng. Mokgatle was reportedly far more interested in the formal education that the missionaries could offer than in their religion – indeed, he himself only converted to Christianity a few years before his death.

Kgosi Mokgatle had travelled to Lesotho and stayed with Chief Moeshoeshoe of the Basotho. It was there that he was impressed by the school system of the Paris Missionaries and decided to accept missionaries into the Bafokeng community. He approached the Hermannsburg Missionary Society (HMS) of Lutheran missionaries. In 1867 Christoph Penzhorn established an HMS station at Saron, on land close to Phokeng bought from Paul Kruger, and paid for mainly by the Bafokeng, in livestock, maize and skins.

Christoph Penzhorn and, later, his son Ernest introduced new Christian beliefs and European practices to the

Bafokeng. This meant that many of the Bafokeng cultural practices like initiation (which was increasingly replaced by confirmation), polygamy, and rainmaking became less popular. But the Lutherans wanted to preserve other aspects of Tswana culture. They taught and preached in Setswana and taught the Bafokeng to read the Bible in Setswana. Many Bafokeng still feel loyal to the Lutherans because they introduced them to schooling.

In 1899 Mr Morrison, an African American, established the African Methodist Episcopal Church (AME), also known as the Ethiopian Church, in Phokeng. Morrison established a day school and taught in English. This was the beginning of the arrival of other Christian groups that competed for the attention of Bafokeng minds and souls.

The Rev. Kenneth Spooner, another African American, arrived in Phokeng in 1913 and established

the Pentecostal Holiness Church Rev. Spooner won over many Bafokeng, largely because he insisted that his congregation speak, and learn to read and write, English. The Bafokeng wanted to learn English, as they saw it as a language that would open up opportunities beyond the Transvaal.

Many years later, during the reign of Kgosi James Manotshe Molotlegi, there was a serious dispute with the Lutheran Church. Kgosi James Manotshe called for a traditional rainmaking ceremony during a period of severe drought. The Lutheran missionary at the time forbade his congregation to attend. This made Kgosi James Manotshe so angry that there was a complete breakdown of relations between the Bafokeng and the Lutheran Church for a period of ten years. During this time members of the Lutheran congregation formed their own church, the African Missionary Society. Today many, predominantly Christian, denominations are thriving in the Bafokeng territory.

BELIEF

Naboth Mokgatle points out that the Bafokeng did not need the missionaries to know God:

❝ The period before the arrival of Europeans is referred to by my tribal people as before literature *(pele-a-lekoal-lo)*; after their arrival, after literature *(morago-a-lekoallo)*. Before the arrival of literature my tribe believed in God. Rain, thunder, storm, droughts and the disasters they suffered to them were acts of God, whom they called *modimo*, meaning 'of the sky above'. They imagined that *modimo* was Mosotho like themselves but beyond their reach, and therefore that between them and *modimo*, whom they could not see and talk to, were their dead forefathers, whom they called *badimo*. Their dead forefathers, whom they could not see and talk to, could somehow meet *modimo* in mysterious ways and talk to him … They worshipped their *badimo* in many different ways, offering sacrifices of food which they imagined pleased them and gave them strength to plead to God for them. ❞

Nkwapa Ramowesi, interviewed in the book Women of Phokeng, agrees:

❝ Here in Phokeng [the missionaries] arrived in 1866 when Phokeng was still backward. However, the people knew about God as it was common for every tribe to know something about God. Even a non-Christian whenever he is in difficulties would be heard saying, "I wish God would help me …" Even our great-grandmothers, who used to put on skins of animals since there were no clothes that we know of today, knew about the existence of God … ❞

SECURING THE LAND FOR THE FUTURE

The arrival of the missionaries opened up new possibilities for the Bafokeng to secure possession of their land. Just after the arrival of the Hermannsburg missionaries in 1867 Kgosi Mokgatle called a pitso, or tribal assembly, where a significant decision was made: **'Farms should be bought, in order that there might be a place where [the Bafokeng] could be buried and where their children could live after them and these farms should be bought in the name of a white man ... Mr Penzhorn, the missionary.'**

In 1868 Kgosi Mokgatle purchased a portion of land (Beerfontein no. 263, portion one) from Paul Kruger, registered in the name of Christoph Penzhorn.

Kgosi Mokgatle's foresight was remarkable. But perhaps even more remarkable was that he had the vision and determination to accumulate the wealth that enabled the Bafokeng to buy their land. Throughout his reign he used every means available to him to ensure that the Bafokeng would have a secure and prosperous future.

Migrant workers returning home from the Kimberley diamond mines.

In 1877 Kgosi Mokgatle sent a regiment of young Bafokeng men to the Kimberley diamond fields to earn money with the aim to buy more farms. They could earn up to one pound ten shillings a month on the mines. Upon their return they each had to hand over £5 to Kgosi Mokgatle. His ability to persuade these men to become migrant labourers and pay over a portion of their wage to buy land points to the respect and popularity he enjoyed among his people and to the fact that this was a tightly-knit community.

As many as 500 Bafokeng men worked on the diamond mines at one time or another. However, many of them died in the process. In later years men were also sent to the gold mines for the same purpose. Kgosi Mokgatle was able to buy more farms.

At the end of the 1800s the Bafokeng owned a total of 23 farms.

Although the Bafokeng formed a very small portion of the black population of the Transvaal at this time, they were responsible for almost 20 per cent of land purchases by all black communities.

A map showing the land that Kgosi Mokgatle had bought by the end of the 1000s.

A RELATIONSHIP OF CONVENIENCE AND CONTRADICTION

It is said that Kgosi Mokgatle's ability to grow Bafokeng wealth had much to do with his relationship with Paul Kruger, a relationship that started when they were both young men living on neighbouring farms. It certainly seems to have been an exceptional one.

Kruger could be harsh in his interactions with the black people of the area. He was strongly opposed to the sale of guns and ammunition to 'coloured persons … we cannot but regard them as the archenemies of the whites … their entire nature is such that as soon as they get that opportunity, they will not allow the whites to stay a day longer in the country.' In spite of this the Bafokeng were able to trade their labour for guns.

In general, the black communities in the Transvaal were afraid of Kruger. In one incident Kruger flogged Kgosi Kgamanyane of the Bakgatla-ba-Kgafela so badly that he and his followers moved out of the area to settle in Botswana. Kgosi Mokgatle himself told the 1871 Labour Commission that he was afraid of Kruger. But Kruger does seem to have had a special concern for Kgosi Mokgatle and the Bafokeng, and Kgosi Mokgatle seems to have found a way around Kruger's prejudice. It is said that Kgosi Mokgatle and Paul Kruger would sometimes sit and drink *mampoer* (distilled spirits) together as friends.

President Paul Kruger of the Zuid-Afrikaansche Republiek (ZAR).

Kgosi Mokgatle and three of his sons – probably (from left to right) Paul, Bloemhof and Ruben

When some local white farmers, unhappy about the fact that the Bafokeng were occupying some of the best farmland, wrote to the president of the Transvaal Volksraad to ask that the Bafokeng be removed from their land, Kruger intervened and they were left alone.

In 1887 two of Kgosi Mokgatle's sons, Paul and Bloemhof, travelled to Holland with Kruger's grandson on a three-year study visit. A personal acquaintance of Paul Kruger provided them with separate accommodation in Holland.

The relationship between Kgosi Mokgatle and Kruger has been described as 'mutually dependent' and 'complex and ambivalent'. What is certain is that it had

In 1877 Britain took political control of the ZAR and hostilities between the Boers and the British grew. Kgosi Mokgatle had to make difficult choices about whom to support.

Kgosi Mokgatle was under pressure from the British, as Paul Kruger knew well. In his memoirs Kruger wrote: 'Magato [Mokgatle] beckoned me into his hut and, when we were alone, said: "I can't give you any horses, for if I did, the English would know it tomorrow. But repeat your request in the presence of my men; then I will refuse, and then you must say, 'Very well, then I will take them by force, if you will not give them to me.' Then I shall say in my heart, 'It is good', but I shall refuse with my mouth." I did so, and took two excellent horses for my return journey.'

HOSTILITIES AND LOYALTIES

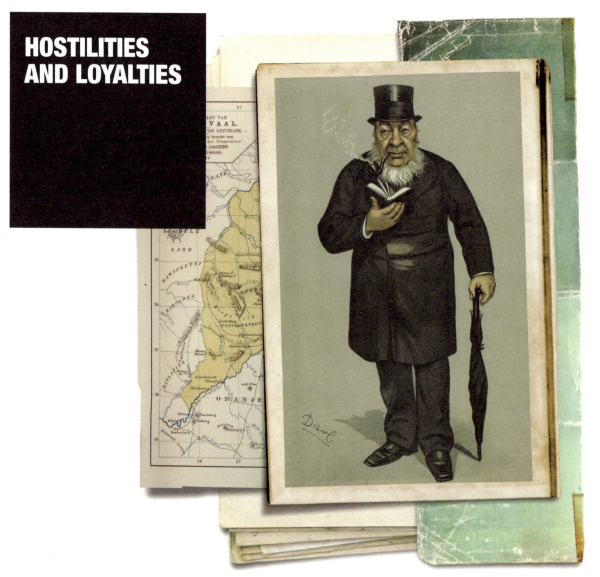

Paul Kruger

Kgosi Mokgatle

On one occasion when Kgosi Mokgatle refused to provide slaughter cattle for the Boers during hostilities with the British in 1881, Kruger grabbed him, threatening to take him prisoner. Kgosi Mokgatle's men immediately threw Kruger on the ground, took his revolver, and then disarmed the other Boers. While Kruger was down, one of Kgosi Mokgatle's men raised his axe and was about to strike him, but the missionary, Mr Penzhorn, who was present, stopped him. Kgosi Mokgatle then ordered the release of Kruger and his men. According to the Commissioner for Native Affairs, who was also present, Kruger went outside laughing, and said to the Bafokeng that they shouldn't get so angry. 'Umkhantla [Mokgatle] and I have grown up together and I cannot harm him.'

NABOTH MOKGATLE GIVES THIS DESCRIPTION OF MOKGATLE IN HIS AUTOBIOGRAPHY: '[MY MOTHER] TOLD ME THAT [MOKGATLE] WAS FEARED AND HIGHLY REVERED BY HIS SUBJECTS... SHE SAID THAT HE WAS EXTREMELY JUST: HE TREATED ALL THE PEOPLE IN THE SAME WAY AND INTENSELY DISLIKED INJUSTICE BEING DONE TO SOME PEOPLE BECAUSE THOSE WHO PROVOKED THEM THOUGHT THEY WERE OF THE LOWER CLASS IN THE TRIBAL SOCIETY HE LOVED CHILDREN AND WOULD NOT LIKE TO HEAR THAT ANY CHILDREN HAD NO FOOD TO EAT... HE WAS A VERY RICH CHIEF... HIS SUBJECTS...REGARDED HIM AS THE FATHER OF THE TRIBE ... OLD PEOPLE IN MY TRIBE STILL SWEAR IN HIS NAME WHEN THEY TESTIFY TO THE TRUTH. THEY CANNOT IMAGINE ANYONE MAKING A FALSE STATEMENT IN HIS NAME THEY ALL AGREE THAT DURING HIS REIGN OVER THE TRIBE NO ONE FELT UNJUSTLY TREATED OR UNJUSTLY JUDGED. THE PEOPLE WHO ARE TERMED COMMONERS ... FELT MORE SECURE DURING HIS REIGN ... HE SAID THAT EVERYTHING HE OWNED BELONGED TO THE TRIBE AND THEREFORE REFERRED TO THEM AS OUR THINGS, OUR CATTLE, OR OUR MABELE CORN.'

44

Kgosi Mokgatle has taught us that mining the future requires two skills that seem almost contradictory: the ability to plan for an imagined future – and the ability to adapt to change.

The ability to plan for an imagined future, on the one hand, is all about staying focused on a goal. It is about determination and perseverance. An example of this is Kgosi Mokgatle's careful planning and unshakeable determination to secure our land.

The ability to adapt to change, on the other hand, is all about knowing when to allow new challenges and opportunities to redefine the way you imagine the future. It is about knowing when to change or even sacrifice old goals for new ones. An example of this is Kgosi Mokgatle's decision to allow missionary education even though it would challenge certain cultural beliefs and practices.

Both of these skills are necessary. Kgosi Mokgatle's wisdom was knowing when to stay focused on the plan and when to change. We learn from him that you can be strong, you can be intelligent, you can even be rich, but if you do not have a plan and you cannot adapt to change, you will not have real power in this world.

Kgosi Mokgatle died in 1891, to this day the longest-serving kgosi of the Bafokeng (57 years).

THE WISDOM OF KGOSI MOKGATLE

MOVING INTO THE 20TH CENTURY

James Tumagole succeeded Kgosi Mokgatle as kgosi but died in 1896 after a short five-year reign. Kgosi James Tumagole is remembered for opposing the system of labour tax, which forced Bafokeng people to work for white farmers without any payment apart from accommodation and food. He ensured that Bafokeng people would never again work for white farmers without receiving proper wages.

His successor, Kgosi August Molotlegi, reigned for 42 years, through some difficult times, including the rinderpest epidemic, which wiped out the Bafokeng cattle herds, and the South African War.

Kgosi James Tumagole

The South African War (1899–1902) has been widely portrayed as a war between the Boers and the British. It is only in recent years that the role of black people in the war has been acknowledged. Hundreds of thousands of black people were dragged into the war against their will. Of all the Pilanesberg communities, the Bakgatla were most involved in the war on the side of the British because of their historical grudges against the Boers.

The Bafokeng were generally regarded as allies of the Boers as they looked after the Boers' cattle while they were on the battlefield. Some were used as scouts by the Boers. It is difficult to establish whether this allegiance extended to the Bafokeng as a whole or was confined to individuals who benefited in very specific ways. On the whole the Bafokeng tried their best to maintain neutrality. Any support they gave the Boers was probably based on practical considerations rather than a sense of loyalty.

[Above] Boer soldiers with black agterryers during the South African War. [Below] British soldiers with black troops during the South African War.

LAND PURCHASES CONTINUE UNDER KGOSI AUGUST MOLOTLEGI

Kgosi August Molotlegi was committed to continue his grandfather's legacy of land purchases. At the beginning of the 20th century the Bafokeng were well positioned to buy more land. They were the largest group in the Rustenburg district with over 9000 people. The more people a tribe had, the more resources it could generate, especially cattle, the major currency used to buy land.

From 1905 to 1913, before the proclamation of the 1913 Land Act, it was possible for black people to buy land in their own name. Kgosi August Molotlegi used this opportunity to buy more farms, which were held in trust by the Minister of Native Affairs. The Land Act did not have quite the devastating impact on the Bafokeng as it did on other African communities, as the land surrounding the Bafokeng was part of a scheduled area where black people were eventually, from 1918, allowed to buy land communally. Kgosi August Molotlegi continued to buy land well into the 1930s. During his reign, 26 farms or portions of farms were registered in the Bafokeng community's name.

Kgosi August Lebone Molotlegi

To this day, most of the land acquired through the efforts of Kgosi Mokgatle and Kgosi August Molotlegi is still held in trust for the Bafokeng community by the Minister of Rural Development and Land Reform. Some families in the Bafokeng region feel that their historical contributions to the land acquisition fund entitle them to private title in the present era, and these disputes have been forwarded to the courts for resolution. What is clear is that the small communities that made sacrifices to enable Kgosi Mokgatle and Kgosi August Molotlegi to purchase land in the late 19th and early 20th centuries paved the way for security of land tenure for much larger numbers of Bafokeng today.

Kgosi August Molotlegi died in 1938 after a long illness related to tuberculosis. He was 71 years old and had ruled for 41 years. He left an important legacy: the land purchases that would secure the future of the Bafokeng. Just how significant these purchases would turn out to be, Kgosi August Molotlegi only started to realise in his lifetime.

Dikgosi and dikgosana from the Rustenburg district meet with Native Commissioners, 1924

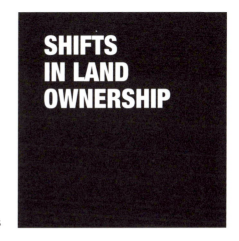

SHIFTS IN LAND OWNERSHIP

It was during Kgosi August Molotlegi's reign that the ore-bearing Merensky Reef was discovered in the Bushveld Igneous Complex, spanning the present-day provinces of North West, Limpopo and Mpumalanga. It is considered to be the most important and most valuable platinum-bearing reef in the world – and a considerable section of the best platinum-bearing ores lies underneath land owned by the Bafokeng.

KGOSI JAMES MANOTSHE MOLOTLEGI

Kgosi James Manotshe Molotlegi with family members at a wedding.

The enthronement of Kgosi James Manotshe Molotlegi.

Kgosi August Molotlegi was succeeded by his son James Manotshe Molotlegi, who reigned for 20 years. These were the early days of apartheid and Kgosi James Manotshe had to contend with a national government that was becoming increasingly repressive. His rule was marked by a number of disputes between himself and the Department of Native Affairs, the Lutheran Church and the mining companies.

One of the landmark court cases of this time involving the Bafokeng was against Rustenburg Platinum Mines (RPM) over mineral rights, based on a contract RPM had signed 27 years earlier with Kgosi August Molotlegi. The Bafokeng eventually won the case on appeal on the basis that, according to the 1913 Land Act, the land in question (Klipfontein 538) fell within a scheduled area where only blacks could own land. In other words, the Bafokeng argued, Kgosi August Molotlegi could not have legally given RPM mineral rights.

This was a significant case among many legal battles that the Bafokeng would fight to keep their rights to their land and the platinum under it.

Kgosi James Manotshe fell ill in late 1955 and died in the Johannesburg General Hospital in 1956. His son Edward Patrick Lebone Molotlegi succeeded him and continued the battle to keep Bafokeng land and mineral rights.

KGOSI EDWARD LEBONE MOLOTLEGI

Kgosi Edward Lebone Molotlegi became kgosi at a very difficult period in South African history. It was the height of 'grand apartheid', with numerous laws designed to separate people politically, socially and geographically.

It was also during Kgosi Lebone I's reign that the exploitation of Bafokeng platinum wealth by the giant mining houses was brought to public attention.

Images of Kgosi Edward Patrick Lebone Molotlegi.

In December 1963 Kgosi Lebone I married Semane Bonolo Khama, a daughter of Tshekedi Khama, then Acting Paramount Chief of the Bamangwato in the Bechuanaland Protectorate. Semane Bonolo, known affectionately as Mmemogolo, or 'grandmother' (having been named after her grandmother Semane), immediately started playing an active role in Bafokeng political life.

In the 1960s and 1970s Kgosi Lebone I pursued major infrastructural developments in the Bafokeng region. The current civic centre was built, roads were tarred, over 20 schools were erected, numerous boreholes were drilled on Bafokeng land, and a health centre and two clinics were erected. In all, about R500 million was spent on capital development in the Bafokeng region during this time with money derived from platinum mining royalties.

APARTHEID

NON EUROPEANS NOT
ADMITTED
RIGHT OF ADMISSION RESERVED
NO DOGS ALLOWED
DO NOT DAMAGE TREES/PLANTS

NATIVES LAND ACT 1913
SPECIFIC CASES.
OF
Evictions
AND

Relations between black and white people in South Africa had already been severely damaged long before apartheid was formally instituted in 1948. The takeover of black people's land by white settlers, and the cattle raids and counter-raids that followed, led to a series of wars of occupation and colonial expansion, as well as mutual suspicion and hostility between white and black. At the end of the 1800s the colonists emerged victorious; South Africa was almost entirely in the hands of the British and the Boers. Socially and territorially, black and white people had been driven apart. Fifty years later this apart-ness was formalised and legalised in the system the world came to know as 'apartheid'.

From 1948 the National Party government officially divided people of different races. Various laws ensured that black and white people could not live in the same areas, marry, or use the same public facilities such as beaches, rest rooms and buses. Other laws forced black people to carry a pass at all times, subjected them to an inferior education system, restricted their ability to work in certain areas, and denied them the vote. Black people became, in effect, non-citizens of South Africa.

The Bantu Authorities Act (No. 68) of 1951 established Bantu tribal, regional, and territorial authorities in the regions set out for Africans under the Group Areas Act, and it abolished the Natives Representative Council. The Bantu authorities were to be dominated by chiefs and headmen appointed by the government. In the early days of the Bantu Authorities Act it was already obvious that the Bafokeng did not want to be part of any Bantustan system. They opted not to become part of another Regional Authority but instead had their existing Tribal Authority declared a Regional Authority. In this way they could retain some measure of independence. The Regional Authority consisted of the kgosi and 84 councillors.

The Bantu Education Act (No. 47) of 1953 decreed that blacks should be provided with separate educational facilities under the control of the Ministry of Native Affairs, rather than that of the Ministry of Education. The pupils in these schools would be taught their Bantu cultural heritage and, in the words of H.F. Verwoerd, Minister of Native Affairs, would be trained 'in accordance with their opportunities in life', which in his view did not reach 'above the level of certain forms of labour'.

'HOMELAND'

In 1972 the various Tswana communities in South Africa were lumped together in the so-called 'homeland' of Bophutha-tswana. According to South African propaganda, this was a 'self-governing state'. The homelands policy operated on the premise that all black people, even those living in urban areas, could only exercise their rights through their respective homeland governments, which meant that all Tswana people, including the Bafokeng, were now so-called 'citizens' of this 'state'.

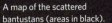
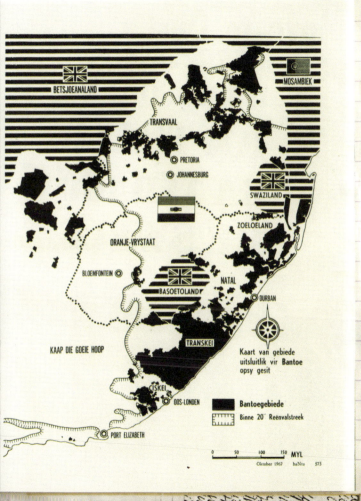

Bophuthatswana was fragmented. It
consisted of seven distinct territorial
units located north or west of the
Witwatersrand and lying near or on
the border with Botswana, with one area
around Thaba N'chu in what was then
the Orange Free State. Bophuthatswana
was entirely dependent on South Africa.
Internationally, Bophuthatswana and
the other 'independent' homelands
(Transkei, Venda, Ciskei) were regarded
as South African puppets and were not
generally recognised.

Because of the platinum mines Bophuthatswana had more material resources
than the other 'homelands'. Nonetheless
it was still largely dependent on funding
from South Africa. Many Bophuthatswana
residents had no access to roads, railways
and telecommunications. Only a third of
its 'citizens' actually lived there.

Dramatic Move to Oust Mangope

KE MOFOKENG KA TSALO, KA TLHAGO KE SWELE.

Chief Mangope

MAIL
INCORPORATING THE MIRROR

MAFIKENG
Tel. 3-3349

FRIDAY, 11th MAY, 1984

REGISTERED AT THE G.P.O. AS A NEWSPAPER
FORMERLY MAFIKENG MAIL, AND BOTSWANA GUARDIAN   ESTABLISHED 1899

PRES. WARNS— WHO SOWS, WILL REAP WAR

President Lucas Manyane Mangope has warned Chief Edward Lebone Molotlegi and the Bafokeng people that "whosoever sows war will reap war." The President said this at a meeting with the tribe and Chief Molotlegi in Phokeng.

The President accused the tribal leaders of damaging the credibility of the Bophuthatswana Government. Wielding a letter which the President said was the result of several meetings held by the tribal leaders in a bid to secede from Bophuthatswana he said they were free to leave the country if they so desired.

He said the Viviers Commission set up to probe into the tribe's affairs had found that the Bafokeng Tribal Authority had not been constituted in accordance with the Tribal Law requirements. Tribesmen had told the commission that they had not been granted

Other points of conflict were:

● The Bophuthatswana flag was not hoisted in the area and Government buildings.

● Government officials including cabinet ministers and magistrates wishing to see Chief

villagers.

ment for the six years of its existence and had failed to give reasons for his absence.

"We have been indifferent to your behaviour for too long," President Mangope told the chief and the tribesmen. "We will not take any action as

President Lucas Manyane Mangope speaking in Phokeng.

Chief Edward Lebone Molotlegi in pensive mood while listening to President Mangope berating him and the Bafokeng Tribe for not adhering to the constitution of Bophuthatswana.

so would automatically be removed as a member

Molotlegi and his counsellors to explain

failed to follow the dictates of the Bophutha.   R2 000 as a reimburs-

The South African government originally offered the position of president of Bophuthatswana to Kgosi Edward Lebone Molotlegi, as he was widely regarded as the most capable Tswana leader of the time. Kgosi Lebone I refused to be a puppet of the apartheid government. Instead Chief Lucas Mangope of the Bahurutshe was instituted as president on 6 December 1977, when Bophuthatswana was granted 'independence'. From that moment on, conflict between Mangope and Kgosi Lebone I grew.

Bophuthatswana was characterised by massive political repression through detention, harassment, dismissals, deportation, torture and sometimes execution. Mangope's regime took action against individuals and political parties that opposed corruption in government circles, such as the National Seoposengwe Party and the People's Progressive Party, making it clear that Bophuthatswana was no place for political opposition. Though presented as a place for all and a haven of non-racism, it discriminated against non-Tswana people by denying them citizenship, work permits and pensions.

Kgosi Lebone I had an automatic right to sit in the Bophuthatswana House of Assembly but chose not to do so. He avoided being sworn in as a member of the legislature and refused to hoist the Bophuthatswana flag in Phokeng. He even destroyed the cheques he received from the Bophuthatswana government as a member of the traditional council. Kgosi Lebone I also refused to carry a Bophuthatswana identity document.

On 3 May 1983 Kgosi Lebone I announced his intention to break away from Bophuthatswana. Mangope responded by declaring a State of Emergency in Phokeng. He went on to appoint a commission of inquiry into the administration of the Bafokeng and to investigate allegations of malpractice by Kgosi Lebone I. What Mangope really wanted, though, was to take over the financial affairs of the Bafokeng in order to access the income from platinum royalties. Mangope could find no evidence of wrongdoing, but tension between Mangope and the Bafokeng continued.

During this time a particular expression became popular: 'Ke Mofokeng ka tsalo, ka tlhago ke swele.' Loosely translated it means: 'I am Mofokeng by birth, by nature I am tough.'

In 1988 Rocky Malebane-Metsing, the leader of the People's Progressive Party (PPP) in Bophuthatswana, and a Mofokeng, attempted to overthrow Mangope in a coup. Mangope's chief of police accused Kgosi Lebone I of being one of the 'pioneers of the coup', even though he was in Johannesburg's Brenthurst Clinic at the time, receiving treatment for a heart condition. A few days later Kgosi Lebone I was detained at the Rooigrond prison outside Mafikeng and interrogated. He was released when the police were served with an urgent court application. Just over a month later, Kgosi Lebone I narrowly escaped rearrest outside his home and fled to Botswana, where he was to spend many years in exile.

In Kgosi Lebone I's absence Cecil Tumagole, his uncle, and the most senior person in the community, was elected Kgosi Lebone I's rightful representative by an overwhelming majority of dikgosana. Mangope was

[Above] Rebel soldiers subdued by the SA Defence Force after the failed coup.
[Below] President Mangope together with apartheid government leaders, Foreign Minister Pik Botha and State President PW Botha.

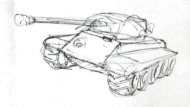

dissatisfied with this. He only wanted Bafokeng who were sympathetic to him in positions of authority. Cecil Tumagole was ousted and George Molotlegi, Kgosi Lebone I's brother, was appointed acting chief. Glad Mokgatle was appointed chairman of the Tribal Council. They were handsomely rewarded by Mangope in the form of business licences, land allocations and commercial opportunities at the new Bafokeng Plaza shopping centre.

After the unbanning of the ANC in 1990, pressure mounted on Mangope to step down, but he formed a political alliance with the white right wing in South Africa and prevented the ANC from operating in Bophuthatswana. However, in March 1994, just weeks before South Africa's first democratic election, Mangope was ejected from power in a popular uprising. Only then did Kgosi Lebone I, Mmemogolo and their children feel able to return to Phokeng.

Protesters in Phokeng during Kgosi Lebone's exile.

Kgosi Lebone I died in November 1995,
not long after his return to Phokeng. His
eldest son, Mollwane Lebone Boikanyo
Molotlegi, known as Kgosi Lebone II,
succeeded him.

NELSON MANDELA SAID AT THE FUNERAL OF KGOSI LEBONE I:

'THROUGHOUT HIS REIGN HE FOUGHT RELENTLESSLY FOR THE DIGNITY AND RIGHTS OF HIS PEOPLE. HIS DEDICATION TO THE SERVICE OF THE BAFOKENG. AND INDEED OF ALL OF THE PEOPLE OF SOUTH AFRICA, EARNED HIM THE HATRED OF THOSE WHO SOUGHT TO ENSLAVE AND SUBJUGATE. HE WAS HARASSED AND HUMILIATED AND FORCED INTO EXILE. BUT KGOSI LEBONE SHOULDERED THAT CROSS WITH DIGNITY AND FORTITUDE. FROM THE OBSCURITY OF EXILE HIS DEFIANT VOICE COULD STILL BE HEARD REVERBERATING THROUGHOUT OUR COUNTRY: "DOWN WITH BANTUSTAN OPPRESSION; FREEDOM FOR MY PEOPLE."'

MMEMOGOLO

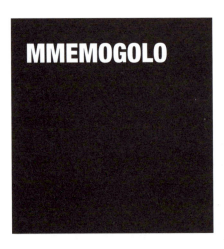

Together with Kgosi Lebone I, Mmemogolo played an active role in the Bafokeng resistance to Mangope. In 1970 she formed the Bafokeng Women's Club (BWC) to promote social activities, Christian education and good fellowship and to raise living standards in the community.

The Bafokeng had always resisted their incorporation into Bophuthatswana, but according to Mmemogolo, 'In the beginning we felt that maybe this was a chance for the person who is going to head Bophuthatswana to use their position for the benefit of the black people and turn things around. But unfortunately it didn't happen that way. This was just somebody who got independence and he felt that he must follow the rules that he'd been given. That's when we started to distance ourselves from Bophuthatswana.'

From 1983 the BWC had continuing run-ins with Mangope, who accused them of setting up the club in opposition to the Bophuthatswana Women's League, headed by Mrs Mangope.

Just after the coup led by Rocky Malebane-Metsing, Mmemogolo was detained with 51 other Bafokeng women of the BWC and held at Rooigrond prison for ten days without being charged. Four months after the coup Mangope banned the BWC from holding meetings, which effectively closed it down.

'WHEN MY HUSBAND WAS IN EXILE I HAD TO CARRY ON.'

While Kgosi Lebone I was in exile in Botswana, members of the Bophuthatswana police continuously harassed Mmemogolo through raids on her home, searches and interrogations, demanding to know the whereabouts of Kgosi Lebone I. In March 1989 she was expelled from Bophuthatswana for not having permanent residency. When she applied for this she was granted only a three-month visa. She went to live with her son Leruo in Johannesburg but frequently returned to Phokeng.

The St Joseph's Roman Catholic mission near Phokeng was situated just outside the Bophuthatswana border and acted as a safe house for Mmemogolo when she needed to meet with people in Phokeng. The mission was also used as a meeting place by the ANC, the National Union of Mineworkers, the People's Progressive Party and the Bafokeng Action Committee. It was harassed by platinum mine management and right-wing farmers and was bombed three times between 1990 and 1991.

RESISTANCE: CHRISTOPHER MAKGALE

Christopher Makgale was one of the founder members of the Bafokeng Action Committee (BAC). The BAC was an attempt to create an alternative to the Mangope-controlled Bafokeng Tribal Council. Mangope's appointee to the Bafokeng Tribal Council, Glad Mokgatle, was perceived as an illegitimate administrator who abused tribal funds.

On 29 December 1990, a group of ten men went to Mokgatle to demand the keys to the Phokeng civic centre. When he refused and allegedly attempted to attack the group with a panga, the panga was taken from him and he was assaulted and fatally wounded. Christopher Makgale was the man wielding the panga that killed Mokgatle.

Christopher was sentenced to 15 years in prison. In 1992 he went on a hunger strike for 76 days in a demand to be recognised as a political prisoner.

In 1996, two years after the reincorporation of Bophuthatswana into South Africa, Christopher successfully applied for amnesty from the Truth and Reconciliation Commission (TRC). At the TRC's very first amnesty hearing he asked Mokgatle's family and the Bafokeng people for forgiveness. He had served six years of his sentence. Today he is a praise singer for Kgosi Leruo.

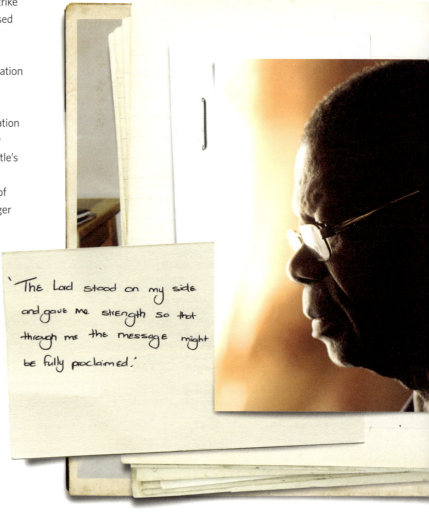

'The Lord stood on my side and gave me strength so that through me the message might be fully proclaimed.'

THAT DAY I WAS PRESIDENT.
I WAS FRIGHTENING. NOW I THINK
I WAS MAD.'

In February 1988 the leader of the People's Progressive Party (PPP), Rocky Malebane-Metsing, attempted to overthrow Mangope in a coup.

Rocky was a Mofokeng who had set up the PPP in consultation with the ANC in exile. According to Rocky, 'We were informed by national politics as led by the ANC at that time. I took several trips to Botswana to meet with ANC leadership. The decision was taken in Kabwe that if the opportunity presented itself we should topple the Bantustan governments by force.'

Rocky was president of Bophuthatswana for less than a day before South African troops came to Mangope's rescue. Rocky went into exile. He returned in 1991 and was elected to the ANC National Executive Committee. 'When we were campaigning in the 1994 elections I met Mangope again in Mmabatho. We wanted to do away with Bop but Mangope was more ruthless than before. It was my daily obsession to bring that regime down. It was the most difficult time of my political career. After a year of hard work Mangope had nowhere to hide – Bop was burning.'

Today Rocky is a local ANC councillor in Rustenburg.

RESISTANCE: ROCKY MALEBANE-METSING

RESISTANCE: MAGGIE BOPALOMO

Maggie Bopalamo, a Mokgatla from Hebron, married a Mofokeng and settled in Phokeng in 1972. She taught at Bafokeng High School, where teachers were forced to take Bophuthatswana identity documents in order to draw a salary. 'Change was forced on us. People were harassed in different ways. If you didn't change your documents, you would lose access to opportunities like bursaries. When parents were targeted by the regime, their children would suffer. I was targeted because of my husband.'

Maggie's husband was an executive member of the PPP. After the coup there was a 'witch hunt'. Maggie was detained with Mmemogolo and others at Rooigrond prison. She was again arrested in June 1988 after returning from a fundraising trip to Harare. She was accused of plotting a second coup in Harare and was placed in solitary confinement for three months before being released on R5000 bail.

Phokeng was divided between supporters of Lebone I and followers of Mangope's ally, George Molotlegi. Suspicion, fear and hatred were rife. Maggie's husband was arrested on treason charges and spent three years in prison. 'Even now he is not recovered ... Phokeng was never the same again.'

VICTORY

'Some problems cannot be solved overnight. After all, apartheid had been reinforced strictly year by year from 1948 onwards. Blacks trapped in their Bantustans received the same message repeated in a thousand different ways: they were incompetent and unfit for national leadership roles because by nature the Bantu were deemed inferior.

Ironically, 1948 was the year in which the United Nations General Assembly adopted the Universal Declaration on Human Rights. The purpose of this declaration was to promote and encourage respect for human rights and fundamental freedoms. The United Nations declaration expounds the personal, civil, political, economic, social, and cultural rights of all regardless of race, creed and colour that are limited only by recognition of the rights and freedoms of others, and of morality, public order, and the common good of all.

Therefore the greatest challenge facing us now is to redeem our own black self-esteem ... A luta continua, the struggle continues, but mainly in our minds. This psychological war within us has to be fought with all our might for our children's sake. It is an even tougher war than the former, but with love and understanding we are sure to gain victory.'

I have always got into trouble for asking questions.

69

THE BAFOKENG TRIBE VS. IMPALA LTD

The Bafokeng are fortunate to hold the mineral rights to 90 per cent of their land.

Impala Platinum, a subsidiary of Gencor, first approached the Bafokeng community authorities in 1966 for a prospecting and mining agreement. This agreement defines all the rights and obligations of both parties, including royalties, once the mining company starts mining. Impala was given the right to mine the First and Second Bafokeng Areas for 35 years, and had to pay the Bafokeng a royalty of 13 per cent of taxable income.

Although Impala made substantial profits and shareholders received generous dividends, the Bafokeng only earned their first royalty from Impala in 1978.

After Kgosi Lebone I went into exile, Acting Chief, George Molotlegi, unlawfully prolonged Impala's right to mine the First and Second Areas, and moreover

granted those rights to them in perpetuity. George also granted Impala the right to mine the Third Bafokeng Area ('the Deeps') in perpetuity, again unlawfully. These were known as the 1990 agreements. These agreements were never approved at a properly convened general meeting of the Bafokeng Community, as they should have been.

Kgosi Lebone I, although in exile, was determined to set aside the unlawful appointment of George and, more importantly, to set aside the 1990 agreements. Thus started a gruelling legal battle.

Kgosi Lebone I and his lawyer James Sutherland of Bell, Dewar & Hall instituted a long-running and ultimately successful legal battle in the Bophuthatswana Courts to set aside the unlawful appointment of George. This was finally achieved shortly after Mangope was deposed and enabled Kgosi Lebone I to resume his leadership of the Bafokeng and return from exile in 1994.

James Sutherland made various attempts to resolve the dispute with Impala regarding the 1990 agreements, both during the reign of Kgosi Lebone I and during that of his successor, Kgosi Lebone II. This included an unconditional and highly favourable offer to Impala that, if it had been accepted, would have resolved the entire dispute. Kgosi Lebone II and Sutherland were stunned by Impala's rejection of the unconditional offer.

COVER

THE BATTLE FOR THE BAFOKENG MILLIONS

The 300 000-strong Bafokeng tribe
would be rolling in money,
but for a bitter battle with
its trustee, Lucas Mangope.
By Ciaran Ryan.

Industrial briefs

700 000 nickel theft

nickel worth R500 00

to appear

Implats is London broker's favoured stock

Record profit for Implats

Impala mining rights row goes to court

Tribe in court bid to court

Impala in battle to

Mining lease intended for I

Tribe has no right to intervene'

Chief alleges govt bias for mine

MAFEKENG — The Bafokeng
tribe of Bophuthatswana last

Bafokeng under fire in court tribe

Impala Platinum

Impala unveils R406m Karee

Impala delays rights offer

Controversy over royalty payments

Impala Mine in court

Bafokeng tribe takes on Impala

7 NOV 1988

SUSAN RUSSELL

The Bafokeng thatswana last court the world's platinum mine, Limited, in a end in the can- mine's right to land.

ispute is whether the contract ced- o Impala is vested r trustee.

tee is the Bophu- President, who is owner of the land. ked the Bophutha- ourt to terminate

Impala MD Donald Ireland said in an affidavit: "Impala was made aware the tribe wished to link negotiations regarding past royalties to the acquisition of prospecting rights in

way

pany to start independent operations on The Deeps, with no infrastructure, shafts or tax shields.
But Molotlegi is investigating several

ee's name did not alter the factual conditions that the tribe owned the land and was fully entitled to deal on its own with its own property.

The President was not empowered to prescribe to the tribe or Impala how the agreement was to be administered or carried out, the chief said.

Figures relating to the mine's operation perhaps indicate how important the outcome of the application is to those directly and indirectly involved. Ireland said the mine's complex include 46 500 people, about 33 400 of these Bophuthatswana citizens. Impala was a major international supplier of platinum and pl

The only reason George has been forced on the tribe, accuses Bogopane, is that Mangope knows he will do the president's bidding whereas Edward would not. Under Edward the Bafokeng tribe not only voted in 1983

In 1995 legal action to set aside the 1990 agreements was therefore instituted against Impala. Impala's case hinged on the argument that the Bafokeng were not the legal owners of their land, an issue that had never been disputed by the Boer, British, Union or apartheid governments.

James Sutherland knew that Impala would be happy to drag the dispute through the courts as long as possible. To counter this he took a strategic decision, known only to himself, to destroy the Impala share price through advertisements in the media that set out the Bafokeng community's side of the story. This strategy worked.

In 1995 a further attempt was made to settle out of court, but the Bafokeng negotiation team saw Impala's stance on the royalties as an act of bad faith and withdrew from the negotiations, a decision ratified by the Bafokeng Supreme Council. The Bafokeng Community published a statement drafted by Sutherland in the *Sunday Times* shortly after they had withdrawn from the negotiations. The Impala share price didn't recover until the final settlement.

In 1998 the courts gave an extremely important ruling that allowed the Bafokeng Community to continue with the case. This ruling, and the advertisements published by the Bafokeng Community subsequent to the ruling, marked the final straw for long-suffering shareholders. James Sutherland addressed all the major shareholders of Impala except Gencor and it was agreed that the Bafokeng demands were entirely reasonable. Sutherland let slip that 'champagne corks would pop' if Impala came to the table. Steve Kearney, the managing director of Impala, seized the opportunity and the matter was settled within months.

The settlement was hailed as a great victory for the Bafokeng. Within a month Impala's share price had tripled and a year later it had increased tenfold.

James Sutherland said: **'Investors can never get enough and this greed can lead to unfair pressure being imposed on the management which can in turn lead to irrational behaviour as we saw with Impala's management. We [the Bafokeng] were never greedy. All we ever wanted was what we perceived to be fair. Kgosi Lebone I, Kgosi Lebone II and the rest of the Bafokeng leadership were principled and brave and enjoyed the overwhelming support of the Bafokeng Community in their battle to ensure that the Bafokeng Community would get what they deserved.'**

The Bafokeng were not the only community to benefit. Kgosi Lebone II, Sutherland and Steve Phiri were instrumental in forming the Mineral Rights Association of Indigenous People of South Africa, in an effort to ensure that other communities had access to resources and information that would equip them to withstand exploitation by mining industry giants.

A HISTORIC JOINT VENTURE: BAFOKENG RASIMONE PLATINUM MINE

The battle against Impala had not yet reached conclusion when the Bafokeng Community entered into negotiations with Amplats (now Angloplat) for a joint venture in respect of the Bafokeng Rasimone Platinum Mine (BRPM). Kgosi Lebone II was determined that the joint venture should be equal and James Sutherland was convinced that a 50:50 joint venture was achievable.

Sutherland and Azhic Basirov, a top financial expert with the London firm Smith & Williamson, entered into a four-year negotiation with Amplats, assisted when necessary by top mining and platinum experts. The joint venture related to the farm Styldrift in respect of which the Bafokeng Community owned the surface and mineral rights, and the adjacent farm Boschkoppie, in respect of which the Bafokeng Community owned only the surface rights, while Amplats owned the mineral rights.

Agreement was reached on 25-year mining plans for a stand-alone Bosch-koppie Mine, a stand-alone Styldrift Mine, and a joint mine. It became clear that the joint mine was worth at least twice the combined value of the two stand-alone mines.

When it emerged that the Bafokeng Community and Amplats had agreed in principle to a 50:50 joint venture Amplats shareholders were enraged, while the financial media reacted with disbelief. Such a deal had never before been concluded.

The BRPM Joint Venture was agreed to in 2002 and was subsequently described by Steve Kearney, who had by then been appointed as the first chairman of Royal Bafokeng Resources, as a 'blueprint for all future deals'. At the end of 2009 the BRPM JV was restructured so that Royal Bafokeng Resources (a subsidiary of RBH) holds a majority interest of 67 per cent and Angloplat's Rustenburg Platinum Mine the remaining 33 per cent.

The latest development in respect of the Bafokeng Rasimone Mine is that the deeper Styldrift component of the mine is being developed. The Styldrift component of the Bafokeng Rasimone Mine will exploit one of the last major Merensky mining blocks on the Western Bushveld.

KGOSI MOLLWANE LEBONE BOIKANYO MOLOTLEGI II
FROM TRIBE TO NATION

Mollwane Boikanyo Lebone Molotlegi II, the eldest son of Kgosi Lebone I, succeeded his father upon his death in 1995. He is known as Kgosi Lebone II. He immediately assumed an active, progressive role in tribal governance and continued to fight the legal battle against Impala.

Kgosi Lebone II was a communications major at Howard University in Washington, DC. **He brought a new perspective to the Bafokeng's role in a modern, global society.** He replaced the terms 'tribe' and 'chief' with 'nation' and 'king' in an effort to restore dignity and status to African communities in the post-colonial dispensation.

He became King Lebone II and the Bafokeng tribe became the Royal Bafokeng Nation. The former Bafokeng tribal authority became the Royal Bafokeng Administration (RBA).

One of the high points of his reign was the announcement of Vision 2020. In Vision 2020 he challenged the Bafokeng people to reduce their dependency on their diminishing mineral assets and become a self-sufficient community by the second decade of the 21st century.

Kgosi Lebone II died in 2000 and was succeeded by his brother Leruo Tshekedi Molotlegi.

King Lebone Molotlegi II

'He made all Africans proud by courageously and consistently reclaiming the birthright that his people had in the minerals that were mined from the belly of the land of his forefathers. And he lived to see his people becoming the first traditional community in South Africa to have a substantial share in the mining company ...

'We are all proud of him for putting to shame all those African leaders who thought, and still think, and act as if the mantle of leadership is a passport to a self-perpetuating life of self-enrichment, divorced from the economic questions facing his people.

'...Unlike many other leaders before him, many of whom would sooner embellish themselves with royal titles in order to elevate themselves to be as far above the status of their subjects as possible, Mollwane regarded every Mofokeng as being equal to all other kings, queens, earls, viscounts, dukes, princes and called them Royal Bafokeng Nation. In his unassuming and quiet style, he enriched the debate around municipal boundaries with fresh ideas, exposing dangers and weaknesses without seeking to usurp the process, but to ensure that all people have a place under the sun.'

THE CHALLENGE OF SKILLS DEVELOPMENT IN POST-APARTHEID SOUTH AFRICA

One of the challenges facing our leaders in a post-apartheid South Africa is to bring our people into the information age and into the global economy in spite of the poor education and the lack of development opportunities during apartheid. One way of making this leap was to hire experienced managers to work towards Vision 2020 and transfer their skills to new generations of Bafokeng professionals. These people were employed because they had the skills and expertise we needed to reach our goals. Many of these people were non-Bafokeng.

Even as qualified Bafokeng increasingly take over the management of Bafokeng institutions, we will always invite people of imagination and intelligence from all backgrounds to help us create our future.

Inside the Royal Bafokeng Administration.

Our culture has not remained the same over hundreds of years. Most Bafokeng today are Christian. This was a fundamental change in our culture. New communication technologies are making it both easier and more crucial for Bafokeng to embrace their role as global citizens interacting with the wider world on a daily basis. The Internet already creates platforms for dialogue that opens us to wider horizons and global perspectives.

Bafokeng culture is a living, learning and growing thing.

Like all living cultures, Bafokeng culture needs to balance the old and the new, the predictable order and the ability to change. We need to preserve traditional knowledge in order for our culture to remain true, and we need to be prepared to change in order to adapt effectively. Rigidly holding to former ways makes our

BAFOKENG CULTURE IS A LIVING CULTURE

culture fragile and easy to damage. Too much change makes it unpredictable and unreliable. We need to know what to keep and what to change, when to challenge and when to show tolerance, when to fight for what we have and when to compromise.

Through all these challenges and changes we have had to face, one thing has not changed: the ability of Bafokeng to adapt.

KGOSI LERUO TSHEKEDI MOLOTLEGI

Leruo Tshekedi Molotlegi did not expect to be kgosi. He had two older brothers. The middle brother, Fosi Boemo Matale Molotlegi died on 17 April 1999, while the eldest brother, Kgosi Lebone II, was still kgosi. Kgosi Lebone II died on 29 March 2000, only five years after being made kgosi. Leruo was then to embrace the role of kgosi in 2000. His enthronement took place on 16 August 2003. Kgosi Leruo completed school at Hilton College in Natal and holds a degree in architecture and urban planning from the University of Natal. He is an accomplished athlete and a fixed wing and rotorcraft pilot, and has been appointed as an honorary Colonel in the South African Air Force.

His inspirational leadership and recognition as a role model have led to his being made the Chancellor of the North West University. He was also the President of the Mineral Rights Association of Indigenous People of South Africa and was one of the principal interlocutors in the Mineral and Petroleum Resources Development Act (No. 28 of 2002), which seeks to encourage significant black participation in the mining and energy sector.

The main message of Vision 2020 is:

SURV!VAL IS NOT ENOUGH!

We have a history of great leaders who were able to use their imagination to create a picture of the future and to use their intelligence to plan towards that future. Kgosi Leruo's challenge has been to take Vision 2020, his brother Kgosi Lebone II's ambitious idea, and make it a reality.

We need to do more than survive. We need to grow in health, wealth, knowledge, skills and enterprise. This plan is not being developed in isolation. It is part of the integrated development plan for the greater Rustenburg area.

It also embraces the vision and spirit of the UN's Millennium Development Goals.

'Inspired by the best legacies of my forebears, we will strive to meet our responsibilities to future generations. We will not shy away from things that may not reward us with an immediate dividend, but that do offer long-term security. We will not address the needs and wants of today at the expense of the long-term interests of the community.'

Kgosi Leruo Tshekedi Molotlegi in his speech at the official opening of the Bafokeng Supreme Council, 18 February 2010

THE FUTURE WILL LOOK VERY DIFFERENT FROM WHERE WE ARE NOW

ROYAL BAFOKENG HOLDINGS

MINING	**Impala Platinum Holdings Limited (Implats)**
	Royal Bafokeng Platinum
	Merafe Resources
MANUFACTURING	**Astrapak**
	Metair Investments
	Bafokeng Concor Technicrete
SERVICES	**Fraser Alexander**
	MB Technologies
	Senwes
	DHL Express
	Mining, Oil and Gas Services (MOGSI)
	Eris Property Group
	Pasco Risk Holdings
	M-Tech Industrial
	Praxima Payroll Systems
	Metuba
FINANCIAL	**Zurich Insurance Company of South Africa**
SPORT	**Platinum Stars Football Club**
	Platinum Leopards Rugby
TELECOMMUNICATIONS	**Vodacom SA**
LOCAL BUSINESS DEVELOPMENT	**Royal Bafokeng Enterprise Development**

Kgosi Lebone II warned us that by 2020 platinum mining will no longer be a growing industry. This means that our economy and the skills of our people have to move beyond mining and become more diversified.

A year before he was enthroned as kgosi, Leruo planted the seeds for what is now Royal Bafokeng Holdings (Pty) Limited, or RBH.

Wholly owned by the Royal Bafokeng Nation, RBH is an investment company responsible for growing and diversifying the community's assets and ensuring a steady flow of income to fund social development. From 2007 RBH started converting some of its royalties into shares. Since then its investment portfolio has grown considerably.

The success of platinum has naturally led to high expectations from the Bafokeng people. For some, Vision 2020 means that we do not have to work hard because our leaders will provide us with jobs and services and dividends. But for Vision 2020 to become a reality, we must all work our hardest and not give up when faced with challenges. We all need to continue to be resourceful and resilient.

We know that we are not an island. The global recession and the drop in the platinum price have had a huge impact on our plans. An example of this can be seen in the 2010 budget of R800 million for all community-based projects of the Royal Bafokeng Nation. This is R400 million less than the 2009 budget of R1.2 billion.

We need to find smart solutions to the challenges before us. Our commitment to increased self-sufficiency is a commitment to education, innovation, environmental responsibility, taking the long view of things and being accountable.

By 2020 the global economy will be centred on innovating and developing new technologies in energy, food security, medicine, communications, transport and architecture, among other things. These new technologies will have to be environmentally friendly and accessible to more of the world's population without compromising research and development, which is expensive and needs to make back its costs.

To participate effectively in this economy we need to make sure that more Bafokeng are well educated, especially in science and mathematics, or we will be left behind.

We have a history of adaptation and claiming for ourselves what works best. Now more than ever we need to be true to this tradition.

At the heart of Vision 2020 is education. Kgosi Leruo's top priority is equipping Bafokeng people for the future, both with skills and with a sense of possibility.

The Royal Bafokeng Institute (RBI) has been created with the specific task of overseeing the education of the nation. It sees itself as 'an engine for change'.

Its work includes:
- managing 45 schools;
- improving school management;
- involving all stakeholders in the planning and decision-making process of schools, including parents, traditional leaders, clergy, school leaders and learners;
- providing state-of-the-art early childhood education for children aged 3–6;
- providing good nutrition for learners in all Bafokeng schools;
- expanding the range of post-secondary options for young adults, both academic and vocational;
- leadership training; and
- supporting the commitment of the dikgosana (headmen) to be lifelong learners.

LEBONE II, COLLEGE OF THE ROYAL BAFOKENG: A CENTRE OF EXCELLENCE

Lebone II College of the Royal Bafokeng has been built on the side of the beautiful Tshufi Hill, overlooking the communities it serves. It is more than a school. It is a centre of excellence and a catalyst for change for the whole Bafokeng community.

Although Lebone II is an independent school, students who qualify through academic merit will pay fees on a sliding scale, and 70 per cent of students will come from the Bafokeng villages.

Classrooms have their own atriums and lounge areas for discussion groups. Kgosi Leruo, with his background in architecture, has been intimately involved in the design. The spaces have been organised in the spirit of a village and embrace the old African maxim: It takes a village to raise a child.

An amphitheatre will be available to the broader community as a meeting space.

A retreat centre hidden on the other side of the mountain in an idyllic landscape will be available for all schools as a destination for workshops and school camps.

Highly skilled teachers have been attracted from leading schools around the world. It is envisaged that this school will become one of the top schools in Africa.

At the heart of it all is a focus on developing a critical educational methodology that will have ripple effects throughout the region.

We view teachers as the most important professionals in our community, and we will see to it that they perform to the highest possible standards, and are afforded the greatest respect and status.

Kgosi Leruo Tshekedi Molotlegi
in a 2007 address

Lebone II will serve as a resource and training centre for principals and teachers in other Bafokeng schools. Classrooms have been designed to accommodate visiting principals and teachers, who will have the opportunity to observe and learn and critically engage with the teaching methodology of the College.

Classrooms are a powerful platform for change and progress, and many more talented Bafokeng will be recruited to teach in our schools in the coming years.

If you have maths, you have the whole world

One of the great Bafokeng success stories of recent times is the unprecedented turnaround for mathematics education in a rural area.

Two of our maths champions are Thabo Mosenyi (now a 2nd-year mechanical engineering student) and Jacob Sello-Khumalo (now a 2nd-year chemical engineering student). After completing school, and before going on to study at Tshwane University of Technology on Bafokeng loans, they both spent an extra year helping high school learners with their maths. They felt that it was important to 'plough back' some of the skills and opportunities that had been opened up for them.

Thabo says, 'Everything is mathematics. If you have maths, you have the whole world.'

Jacob says that maths has changed the way he sees the world. 'Maths has given me another sense.'

Jacob fell in love with maths in Grade 5 and really believes that succeeding at it is all about attitude. He believes that each choice he makes and each step he takes contributes to shaping his future. 'The path you take determines your destination.'

Thabo says that there are many things that distract young people from succeeding, such as worrying about money and feeling pressured to socialise. But the greatest obstacle, according to him, is believing that you are not capable. He said, 'I would say to young people: Go in with all your heart and don't look back. Don't have doubt. Maths will give you a bright future.'

Jacob says that being Mofokeng 'is a wonderful thing … it gives you the opportunity to be what you want to be, it gives you the idea that you can come out of your circumstances.'

Thabo says that what is most important is 'Knowing what you want, knowing where you come from, knowing where you're going to.'

Maths can give you anything, take you anywhere.

Jacob Sello-Khumalo
and Thabo Mosenyi

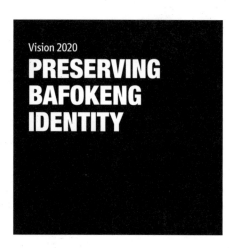

Vision 2020

PRESERVING BAFOKENG IDENTITY

By 2020 there will be new challenges to preserving our Bafokeng identity.

We need to support those people who are committed to creating, adapting and preserving Bafokeng culture, whether they are artists, designers, performers, storytellers or historians.

Many other groups in South Africa have a distinctive material culture. In other words there are traditions of architecture, wood carving, bead working, weaving and painting that are very recognisable as Venda, Ndebele, Zulu and so on. These traditions can also be used as evidence for understanding the history of these groups. The best example we have of an artistic tradition that is still alive is our traditional dancing.

But if you look around Bafokeng territory you will not see other traditional Bafokeng artistic traditions. Our architecture, beadwork, basket weaving and ceramic traditions have been lost. Even a Bafokeng tradition of healing is growing weaker.

While we have kept our traditional leadership structures, we have unfortunately lost most of our material culture.

HOW DID WE LOSE SO MUCH OF OUR MATERIAL CULTURE?

The conflict of the Difaqane left Bafokeng traditions very vulnerable to change. When Kgosi Mokgatle returned to Phokeng in 1836 many traditions were already fragmented and vulnerable to outside influences like that of the Christian missionaries.

Church practices and lifestyles popularised certain cultural trends, such as European architecture, Western dress, and eating with knives and forks.

Church confirmations were held among the same age groups previously enrolled in traditional initiation rituals *(bogwera* and *bojale)*. This change was so successful that young Christians even asked the kgosi to give their confirmation group a name, just as he always named age regiments *(mephato)* for initiation. He agreed. Circumcision and initiation were eventually abandoned during Kgosi August Molotlegi's reign in 1905.

Maggie Bopalamo reflects on the influence Christian missionaries had on Bafokeng culture in her book *Phenyo – Victory:* 'Ancestral devotions and most forms of traditional healing were regarded as forms of paganism. Little did people realise that they were made to throw away what they really were, and that they were left with nothing that could be called their own, nothing to be proud of as black people. Later in life they would regret they allowed this to happen.'

While some feel that Bafokeng traditions are dying, others are living proof that tradition is alive and well.

Mmantshope Pitsoe is a praise singer from Kgale village and a Mofokeng by marriage. She has been responsible for praising the legacy of many Bafokeng dikgosi. She learnt the art from her grandmother and is teaching it to her grandson, Kearabetswe Pitsoe.

'I must pass on knowledge before I pass on … Every gift I have I want to pass on – add on to what people already have … Our own children do not have a memory for old traditions and skills.'

Kearabetswe is determined that he will carry on the tradition.

**I must
pass on
knowledge
before
I pass on**

Here are three generations of praise singers: Kearabetswe Pitsoe, his grandmother, Mmantshope Pitsoe, and an image of her grandmother.

'Praise poetry is a gift you can't keep to yourself.'

This praise poem focuses on the myth of the crocodile that the Bafokeng encountered at Mmakhunyedi – and made their totem. 'The crocodile is praised by the Sons of the Soil. It is praised by the Bafokeng of Phokeng.' It is described as 'one who can run very fast,' 'a vehicle to the battle field,' 'with a sharp ear to hear all the gossip.' Like most praise poems there are references to history creating a context. The suffering under Mzilikazi is remembered, but the crocodile offers strength for the Bafokeng to climb Tshufi Hill, to climb towards success.

LEBOKO LA BAFOKENG BA PHOKENG

Kwena ga ke boke ke a okaoka;
Ke boka ke boifa Moselekatsi wa Mashobane;
Ba ntlha ya tlase ga ke ba boife;
Ba ntlha ya tlase ga nke ba boka;
Kwena e bokwa ke ntlha ya godimo;
E bokwa ke Bafokeng ba Phokeng;
Rona basimane re a kekologa.

Dididmalang jalo bafokeng;
Tlhwaang ditsebe lo reetse thata;
Lo utlwe fa ke golodika phalafala;
Kwena e maoto a makokoma;
Tshesebe e e mo maisa ntweng;
Yo o maoto a a bofefo go siana;
Yo o tsebe ntlha go utlwa ditshebo.

Tlhwaang ditsebe basimane ba kgosing;
Lo tlhwae ditsebe lo reetse thata;
Lona ba dintlha ga ke le umake;
Ke bua le basimane ba kgosing;
Lo rileng kwena lo phakela;
Mme tlhaang ke utlwa kwena e galefile;
Ke utlwa kwena e kgalema ke le kgakala;
Ke itlhoma ke palama Thaba ya Tshufi;
Ke raya fa phateng ya Mabudu;
Gaufi le sope la Matebele;
Gaufi le lengope la Mmakhunyedi.

Once you know yourself you can fulfil history

Tshepang Maelangwe is a Rastafarian artist who is passionate about being a Mofokeng and has said that 'being a Mofokeng is about being the best in Africa'.

'Get to know yourself before looking to others'

While Tshepang values individuality, he sees the leadership structures and cultural traditions of the Bafokeng as a system that has developed over many years and has proved to be reliable. He said, 'Bafokeng culture is the things we do day to day, like the protocol we follow as Bafokeng: the way we greet, how we behave around funerals and marriages, the way we communicate with our king, the way we ask visitors to first report to the kgosana, our respect for elders …'

He challenges the Royal Bafokeng Nation to provide more opportunities and support for artists, but he is not waiting to be rescued by anyone. Even with few resources he works relentlessly to produce artworks and to continue developing his skill.

Tshepang challenges other young people to take control of their future. 'Before taking Vision 2020 seriously, take yourself seriously. Everything else will follow. Once you know yourself, you can fulfil history.'

Kagiso Mogale didn't get to where he is because of money or social networks. Born in Kanana, he went to Johannesburg after Grade 5. His mother passed away and his father left him. Out of sheer determination he found his way on to the television drama *Generations*. 'I had so much passion for the entertainment industry that I was willing to volunteer to get the chance to show what I can do.'

He then started writing for television soaps and eventually became part of the team that produced *Tsotsi*. He is now developing a film called *How I Met Majita* – a love story in a gangster-ridden township.

'I am proud to be a Mofokeng. I made a decision to come back to North West because I wanted my film to be a Royal Bafokeng film, I wanted to be the guy to open up film production in Royal Bafokeng.

'Too many young people feel we are in the "wrong" province ... where nothing happens. North West people are still trying to find their feet. I have met lots of passionate, driven people here. We should be our own leaders, stand up and do it for ourselves.'

'THERE IS NO SUCH WORD AS IMPOSSIBLE.'

Stand up and do it for yourself!

A picture is worth a thousand words

Mogale Mogale is multi-talented. He is a photographer, a graphic designer, a self-taught IT systems architect and a music producer. He was awarded the Moses Kotane Municipality award for best service provision in the region.

He started out studying advertising at the Vaal Triangle Technikon. He worked for two years with an IT engineer, learning on the job before joining Leo Burnett advertising agency for four years. Then in 2000 he started working solo as a designer. He designed brochures for the World Summit on Sustainable Development under contract to Amos Masondo, the mayor of Johannesburg. He also did work for Gold Reef City Casino. And yet all this success could not keep him away from Phokeng. 'Coming home was the best decision I ever made. In Johannesburg I did commercial advertising but now I do more meaningful work. This is my territory. I understand it better than anything.'

Royal Bafokeng Administration (RBA) is one of his main clients. His first job for the RBA was the enthronement of Kgosi Leruo. He works closely with Johnny Taute from I-Line Media.

Mogale spends as much energy as he can on traditional music production. 'It is very me.'

MY ROOTS SHOW!

Johannes 'Big John' Swaratlhe used to be a hairdresser but has transformed himself into a performing artist.

He started doing kwaito in 1997. 'Then I heard Tsepo Tshola singing and I couldn't sleep. I thought, this is the kind of singing I should do. When my pastor heard me sing he bought me a keyboard. People started coming to hear me and this church was built.'

One day he went to hear Princess Tirelo preach. She asked somebody to sing. 'I felt a calling. I sang that song, *If I believe and you believe, then Bafokeng will be saved*. The princess loved the song … When she returned from a trip to America she asked me to usher her into the Bafokeng stadium with that song … It was the first time I saw Kgosi [Leruo] at close range. I was scared, but the princess was so happy to see me. Since then I have sung with the big guys, with Gloria Bosman, Umoja, etc. I even sang at the Kgosi's enthronement.

'I get no income from singing. My parents support me but it is difficult. I have a one-year-old child. Sometimes it stresses me because it gets in the way of my creative juices. I would like to live from my talents.'

'Something wonderful happens when I Sing!'

Finding a voice

Vision 2020

THE POWER OF SPORT TO UNIFY A NATION

More than ten years ago Kgosi Lebone II said that we would witness international sport in our own backyard. The dream has come true. We have already hosted a number of international teams in our community-owned stadium, the Royal Bafokeng Sports Palace. We can also be proud of the fact that we are the only rural community that will be remembered as a venue for the 2010 FIFA World Cup.

Our Bafokeng leaders have recognised the power of sport to unify a nation. Sport not only offers the opportunity of attaining health and physical fitness in the form of recreation, but it also promotes the values of discipline, team spirit, self-esteem and a commitment to continuing self-improvement. These are values vital to Vision 2020. Royal Bafokeng Sports (RBS) manages this vision. The RBS managing director George Khunou says: 'We realised the importance of sports in awakening and motivating people. And once we decided to go with it, there was no place for half-measures.'

Royal Bafokeng Sports owns two professional teams: the Platinum Stars (PSL) and the Platinum Leopards (Currie Cup Rugby). In the villages, there are more than 20 000 children participating in athletics, martial arts, netball, rugby and soccer. Khunou says: 'The plan is for them to have a shot at the senior team one day.'

We have also turned sport into a business opportunity through our world-class 65-hectare training facility called the Bafokeng Sports Campus. Here teams from all over the world will come to train on its state-of-the-art training pitches and enjoy the luxurious five-star accommodation of the Royal Marang Hotel secluded in the bushveld far from distractions. It also includes a high-performance gym with medical facilities. The real attraction is the opportunity to train at the ideal training altitude of 1200 metres. The Sports Campus will not only cater for professionals but will also accommodate promising young sportsmen and women.

Our sports facilities are a flag that will put us on the world map and draw attention to Vision 2020 and our commitment to development through innovation.

THE INFRASTRUCTURE OF DEVELOPMENT

By 2035 the Royal Bafokeng Nation's population might double to 700 000 people. This means that the need for services will grow.

We need to build on the legacy of Kgosi Lebone I and improve our infrastructure. The Masterplan outlines an integrated way of doing that over the next twenty-five years.

Commercial, industrial and residential electricity needs will grow beyond what is currently being provided by Eskom. RBN will have to work together with Eskom to upgrade the existing network and eventually install new facilities.

RBN purchases water from Rand Water and Magalies Water and provides it to us at subsidised rates. We are also going to have to learn how to save, store and recycle water properly so that there is a cost-effective source for everyone. The average rainfall in our area is sufficient to meet almost 50 per cent of our domestic and industrial needs including agriculture.

We need to harvest and store rainwater effectively.

Our waterborne sewerage system is being built and every household will have a flush toilet by 2012. Later, we will expand that system through the introduction of regional sewage treatment plants to deal with the increased demand.

As far as waste management is concerned, a local garbage collection service will be introduced with the assistance of the Rustenburg Local Municipality. New landfill sites and transfer stations will also be constructed. Hand-in-hand with this will be a continuing education campaign to raise awareness of the importance of reducing, reusing and recycling refuse to ease the pressure on landfills. Our region could even become a centre for recycling technology in North West Province.

We have developed one of the best road networks in any rural area. Roads will need to be upgraded and widened and new roads built to handle increased traffic. We want to make all areas more accessible so that entrepreneurs and small business owners can operate more effectively. A bypass will be constructed to divert heavy traffic away from Phokeng and the other villages. Bicycle lanes will be introduced to encourage cycling and reduce traffic volumes in the residential areas. A more efficient public transport system will be introduced with bus terminuses in every village.

We also need to focus our energies on developing more diverse housing options for everyone in our community.

By 2035 the health needs of our community are going to increase.

The health challenges we face are not unique to our community. The provision of accessible, affordable and effective health care and social services remains one of the greatest challenges throughout South Africa.

What makes these challenges different for us?

We are a small community. We have unusual resources. We know our leaders personally. We have prioritised education as the most important aspect of development. For all these reasons, we are in a great position to have honest conversations about the spread of HIV, exploitation of young girls by sugar daddies, teenage pregnancies, the abuse of alcohol and domestic violence. These are things we should be able to talk about in our homes, with our friends and colleagues, with the management of Royal Bafokeng Nation institutions, with our dikgosana and with our Kgosi.

RBN is in the process of:

- renovating clinics;
- increasing the number of medical personnel;
- extending the range and reach of medical services through mobile clinics;
- managing a fleet of ambulances with a satellite ambulance station in Kanana;
- establishing an Emergency Medical Service Centre with a call centre;
- providing food and support to orphaned and vulnerable children;
- organising school feeding schemes;
- reducing reliance on government grants through skills development and job opportunities;
- empowering disabled people in the spirit of our motto, 'Independent living for people with disabilities';
- caring for the elderly;
- improving access to and services at pension pay-points;
- creating sports facilities that offer a wide range of healthy recreational activities.

The challenge for all Bafokeng is to become more aware of these initiatives, find out all we can about them, support them and hold our leaders accountable for maintaining them.

FOOD SECURITY

By 2035, food security will be a bigger challenge than it is now, as there will be more people and less land to farm on.

Food security is one of the greatest challenges facing the world. Agriculture is in crisis in South Africa. Small commercial farmers have been hard hit by the economic recession and land reform laws. Much of our own agricultural land has been taken over by mining. Traditional knowledge systems for farming are disappearing fast. Not many young people see farming as an attractive career choice. A skill that was so fundamental to the survival of our ancestors is now being lost.

Royal Bafokeng Enterprise Development (RBED) has therefore provided training for a group of highly motivated entrepreneurs who want to start an agribusiness. RBED rents out greenhouses to them on what used to be Paul Kruger's old farm, Boekenhoutfontein. The greenhouses were developed through corporate social investment funding by Senwes, the second largest agricultural services company in the country. Part of this funding is given to entrepreneurs in the form of loans. When these loans are paid back, the money circulates to other projects.

Like all entrepreneurs in South Africa they face many challenges but have not given up.

As they say, 'We have discovered that cucumbers and rosa tomatoes are not very popular in nearby markets. We need to do a better feasibility study before choosing seeds for our new crops … We also need to think more about how to work out our prices … Transport is a big problem. It is very expensive and unreliable. Sometimes vegetables lie rotting before we can get them to the market … Packing our produce is difficult because we don't have any covered space. We have to work under the trees. When it rains we are in trouble.'

With clients like Sun City, these entrepreneurs are encouraged to persevere.

Their efforts are not just for themselves. They employ nine assistants who help with the planting, picking and pruning. The assistants always get paid first. If there is any money left over after paying costs at the end of the month, these young entrepreneurs may be able to pay themselves R1000 each. They feel it is worth it because they are building a skills base and a business.

William M. Mquthe, Mark Abel Rakgomo, Salome Rakgokong and Sam Boitumelo Patshoane working in one of their greenhouses.

'It takes time to grow something beautiful.'

ENVIRONMENT

By 2035, if we continue the way we are now, the environment will be so damaged that we will not be able to use it to plant food or attract tourism.

In so many ways, we are who we are because of our land. The way we secured our land, our communal ownership of the land and our mineral rights are what set us apart from other communities in South Africa. The harsh reality is that the health, beauty and sustainability of our land is being threatened by economic recession, global warming, the loss of biodiversity, the invasion of alien species, as well as environmental damage due to mining and development. Now more than ever we need to think critically and creatively about the way in which we are going to care for our land.

In the implementation of Vision 2020 all development initiatives are considered together and resources are used in a more sustainable way.

Bafokeng wealth has a shadow side. Mining has long-term consequences for the environment and our health. We need to face these challenges head-on. Platinum mining creates pollution. Toxins from slimes dams get into the streams and rivers, and poisonous gases threaten to increase the number of respiratory diseases in our communities. The buffer zones around slimes dams protect communities, but they also reduce the amount of agricultural land.

If we cannot care for our environment, we will also experience more floods and increased health problems due to poor water quality and malnutrition.

We need to rehabilitate areas that have been affected by mining and turn them into beautiful and safe recreational areas. We are in the process of designing strategies to preserve what natural areas remain and encourage people to value them. Hiking trails and other attractions are planned.

Leaving good footprints

The enthusiasm of Mr Philly Khunou, Corporate Social Investment Director of Bafokeng Rasimone Platinum Mine (BRPM), is truly infectious. 'My job is to develop the communities surrounding the mine and ensure that they benefit from the mines. I am a man who believes in leaving good footprints – I am proud when I leave something behind that I can touch, that I can show.'

One example of the corporate social investment (CSI) that Philly pioneers is the assistance that BRPM has given with the design, funding and furnishing of offices for traditional authorities in the villages of Robega, Rasimone, Chaneng and Mafenya. These offices give a formal base to headmen – a place where locals can submit suggestions and requests and where outsiders, out of respect and protocol, can make themselves known when they visit.

The reality is that the economic recession and the fall in the price of platinum has had an impact on corporate social investment. Anglo Platinum's CSI budget has dropped from R59 million in 2008 to R18 million in 2009 and will drop to R13 million in R2010.

'WE TAKE OUR ENVIRONMENT SERIOUSLY.'

'WE ARE DOING IT FOR OURSELVES!'

If you travel to the village of Chaneng you will find an enormous community food garden that is tended by the Chaneng Association for the Blind. This is a product of the kind of encouragement and support that Philly Khunou has inspired Anglo Platinum to offer the community. He says, 'We count ourselves privileged to be able to support the Chaneng Association for the Blind. It is distressing to see how few people in the rural villages of North West Province plant their own food. The Chaneng Association for the Blind displays the kind of passion for excellence that we want to support.' Good nutrition, provided by community food gardens like this one, is a key to proper brain development in early childhood and to fighting disease. Food gardens also give communities a sense that they are taking control. In this way they facilitate a sense of community pride.

Ntebe Sedikwe, coordinator of the Chaneng Association for the Blind, proudly shows off some of the onions they have grown in their community food garden.

THE VALUE AND THE CHALLENGE BROUGHT BY MIGRANT LABOUR

All through our history our ancestors have always shown a willingness to welcome and accommodate those who are in need, whether they are Bafokeng or not.

In the period from the 1960s to the 1980s there were many non-Bafokeng who made applications to the dikgosana for Bafokeng membership. If your application to become a Mofokeng was approved, you had to give up your allegiance to your previous place of residence, even if that meant changing the way you dress, speak or build your house. You also had to obey other prohibitions like not making a noise at night. You had to get an official transfer from one traditional leader to your new one. You also had to pay kgotla fees and attend local funerals and weddings. You were, however, allowed to continue making sacrifices to your own ancestors, and some people continued circumcision without problems.

Bafokeng identity used to be more flexible than it is today. Today it has become more fixed as it is a marker of rights to some very valuable land, services and loans.

Mines on our land have attracted non-Bafokeng people from all over southern Africa, some to work on the mines and others to trade with salaried mine workers. The Bafokeng territory contains the single largest Mozambican community outside Mozambique.

Migrant labour, throughout the world, disrupts families and communities, both where they come from and where they work. Because of the nature of their lifestyle, migrants are more vulnerable to HIV than most people. This means they are one of the sources of HIV in our communities. They have also contributed to the growing sex industry and the increase in teenage pregnancies.

Having said this, we do owe a lot to these people who have helped us access the wealth beneath us. We need to think carefully about how we show our gratitude and accommodate them within our community.

I followed a dream: I didn't want to regret the choice I made

Tebogo Molefe is a prize-winning designer who compares the qualities of the Bafokeng people to the qualities of platinum. 'Platinum is rare and long-lasting. It is hard to work with but it is flexible and does not age. Unlike silver it doesn't break off when scraped or bumped. It remains intact even if it tears. Also, unlike silver jewellery, platinum jewellery is very pure at 95–100 per cent. Platinum is also used as a catalyst in many technologies. It makes things happen but doesn't lose itself in the process.'

Tebogo's jewellery design is informed by traditional Tswana patterns. He won the first annual Platinum Provincial Craft Design Award, awarded by the North West Craft and Design Institute, for a beautiful neckpiece.

Tebogo went to Sekete IV High School. His parents paid for his studies in jewellery design and manufacture at Wits Technikon. The Royal Bafokeng Economic Board then sponsored his BTech at University of Johannesburg. He now teaches at Orbit Further Education and Training College.

'My father wanted me to study metallurgy and go into mining but I followed my own path. I realised the minerals from our soil produced the jewellery I liked. My father is now proud that my career choice has been a success.'

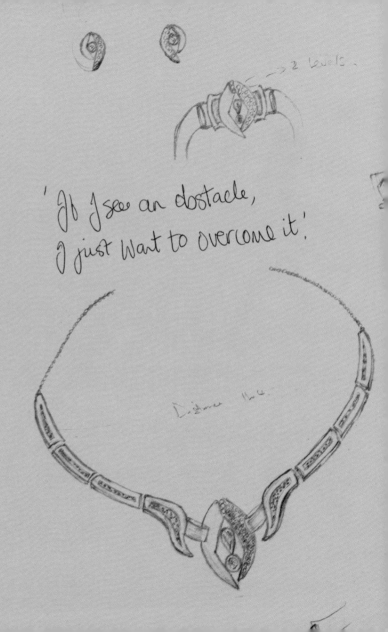

'If I see an obstacle, I just want to overcome it.'

Mmamothofela is a restaurant at the Bafokeng Plaza. It is run by entrepreneur extraordinaire Bertha Nkala Mfulwane. She has two other retail points for her food businesses, one at Xstrata chrome mine and another at the taxi rank in Rustenburg. She is an example of someone who has had very little help on her path to success.

'I only reached Standard Two at school, but I'm doing better than people with schooling.

'I started very small. I was patient – I was prepared to spend time to build my business.'

'I started in 1974 selling vetkoek and soup to children at school. I used a wheelbarrow to take the vetkoek to school. I sold the vetkoek for 1 cent and made R18 a day. I saved all my cents. I struggled. I married and settled in Tlaseng. From 1974 to 1998 I sold fried chicken at the mines. I started by charging R5 for half a chicken. Eventually I was making about R1000 a day. We weren't allowed to sell there and the police would often chase us away. One day was terrible. Police came from all sides and caught everyone. I ran down to the river and hid in the water.

'In 2003 there was an auction at the mine. I didn't have any money but I said, "Let's go, God will help me." I bought a container for R70 000. I said I'd pay cash but I didn't have the money. I asked my family. I also phoned a few close friends and business people and they loaned me money. It took me five months to repay all my loans. I worked hard.'

Her patience, her focus on quality and her ability to invest her profits back into her business helped her grow from strength to strength. She now owns a shop at the Plaza and even caters for Kgosi Leruo and Kgotha Kgothe. She has started diversifying her business and has shares in a taxi business called Golden Rewards.

'I have three sons and a daughter. All my sons can cook. All of them help in the business.'

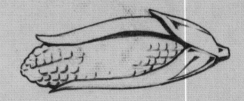

The work is in your hands and your minds.

I was prepared to spend time to build my business

Being an inventor takes a lot of patience

Comfort Mosala Segoe is an inventor.

After being employed for ten years and one failed business venture, he decided to follow his passion and become an inventor.

'My product is a multipurpose safety helmet with seven different features that can be used one at a time or all together depending on the job. Currently no safety helmet has all these features. It can be used in the mining sector, manufacturing, agriculture, cleaning and others.

'Being an inventor takes a lot of patience. It took nine years and nine months for me to design the product. The Product and Development Technology Station in Bloemfontein then helped develop the helmet from idea to prototype. The prototype was then tested by the South African Bureau of Standards. The product failed the absorption test in March 2009 and was retested that July. This time the product failed the electrical insulation test, which it had actually passed in March. The product was finally approved on 4 December. Now I am waiting to hear from the patent attorneys. If things go according to plan I will produce my first product on 3 May.

'During the development of this product, I started 20 others, which I will continue to develop as soon as this product is launched.

'I would say that my success has to do with determination, interest, and belief in the value of what I was doing. I would be able to create jobs for other people and my children would live with benefits from the product forever.

'My wife supported me for ten years. People did not understand. I kept updating my wife so she knew what I was doing. I have learnt that women are capable of doing anything that men can do. I would not even object to a female kgosi.'

Comfort has played many leadership roles in the church, the National Union of Mineworkers, the governing body of his children's school and the local committee that deals with the management of funeral services and other community issues.

'I am proud of being Mofokeng. The reason why I play so many different roles is because I support the vision of Kgosi. He wants to see people in a certain way by 2020. I have been involved in lots of developments for the clan, transforming from old ways into the new.'

Comfort Segoe's helmet, with face visor; welding feature; manifold that supplies air inside the helmet; neck protection; fire and water resistant material; ventilation that can be opened or closed and dust flange.

RSA Design NO: A2010/00624, F2010/00623, A2010/00626, F2010/00625, A2010/00627, F2010/00622